KEYS TO THE HEARTS OF YOUTH
REASON, RELIGION, KINDNESS

St. John Bosco's Pastoral and Educational Mission
A Spirituality and Methodology

Paul P. Avallone, SDB

Salesiana Publishers
New Rochelle, New York
1999

By Paul P. Avallone, SDB

Don Bosco and His Preventive Technique in Education, 1958
Revised in 1965 and 1977 under the title of *Reason, Religion, Kindness: The Educational Method of St. John Bosco*

Copyright © 1999 by Salesiana Publishers, Inc., New Rochelle, New York

All rights reserved. No part of this book may be reproduced or transmitted in any form or by any means, electronic or mechanical, including photocopying, recording, or by an information storage and retrieval system, without permission in writing from the publisher.

Book produced by GGP Publishing, Inc., Larchmont, New York

ISBN 0-89944-376-1

Printed in the United States of America
10 9 8 7 6 5 4 3 2 1

In memory of:

The Seventh Successor of St. John Bosco
Very Reverend Egidio Viganò
1926–1995

He led us to rediscover
The New Preventive System.

In gratitude to:

My parents, who lovingly and wisely
led me along the path of
Reason, Religion, Kindness.

> *Ricordatevi*
> *che l'educazione è cosa di cuore,*
> *e che Dio solo ne è il padrone,*
> *e noi non potremo riuscire a cosa alcuna,*
> *se Dio non ce ne insegna l'arte,*
> *e non ce ne dà in mano le chiavi.*

Remember
that education is a matter of the heart,
and that God alone is its true Teacher,
and that we cannot succeed
unless God gives us the skill
and hands us the keys.

—St. John Bosco

CONTENTS

	Acknowledgments	xi
	Introduction	1
1	Today's Youth, Tomorrow's Leaders	7
2	A Man Sent by God Whose Name Was John	19
3	The Early Apostolate	31
4	Don Bosco in the History of Education	48
5	Reason: Being Reasonable with the Young	56
6	Religion: Walking with the Young to Christ	67
7	Kindness: Reaching the Hearts of the Young	87
	Conclusion: Don Bosco's Contribution to Education	98

SEMINAL DOCUMENTS: APPENDIXES A–C

	Introduction	107
A	The Preventive System in the Education of the Young	109
B	The Use of Punishments in Salesian Houses	117
C	Letter from Rome	130

Acknowledgments

I am indebted to the Very Reverend Timothy Ploch, SDB, Provincial of the Eastern Province of the Salesians of St. John Bosco. He made it possible for me to spend three semesters at the Institute of Salesian Studies in Berkeley, California. I am grateful to the faculty and Community of Don Bosco Hall. Two professors of this Institute are to be singled out for their help, encouragement, and guidance. Rev. Arthur Lenti, SDB, and Rev. Michael Ribotta, SDB, gave invaluable help in the preparation of this manuscript. Likewise, the author wishes to express his gratitude to Sister Mary J. Mullaly, FMA, for her constant encouragement and kind direction.

My sincerest thanks to a number of lay teachers, Salesian Sisters, and my Confreres for reading the manuscript and making valuable comments. Finally, I wish to thank my Confreres Rev. James Hurley and Rev. Philip Pascucci for helping to make the manuscript ready for publication. I express my deep appreciation to Ms. Generosa Gina Protano, of GGP Publishing, Inc., of Larchmont, New York. Her careful and patient expertise brought this manuscript to production.

My deep gratitude to the Salesian Community of Don Bosco Tech, Paterson, for agreeing to allow me to take time for the research and for carrying my responsibilities during my absence.

Lastly, sincerest thanks to my sister, Mrs. Mary Avallone Oropallo, for her generosity in financing this new book on St. John Bosco to whom her husband, Salvatore, was very devoted and who made the name of the Blessed Friend of Youth known in his parish of St. Philip Neri, Bronx, New York.

Don Bosco Tech
Paterson, New Jersey
January 31, 1999

Introduction

In 1988 Pope John Paul II wrote a public letter to the late Very Reverend Egidio Viganò, the Superior General of the Salesians of Don Bosco, on the occasion of the centennial celebration of the death of St. John Bosco. The letter was entitled *"Juvenum Patris"* (Father of Youth). Pope John Paul highlighted the unique contribution made to the Church and to society by St. John Bosco through the educational method he created and called the *preventive system*. The Holy Father urged all the members of the Salesian Family to rediscover this innovative approach and make efforts to update and renew this reaching out to the hearts of youth, using the oft-repeated expression of Don Bosco, "Education is a matter of the heart."

> The figure of St. John Bosco, the friend of youth, continues to exert a fascinating attraction for young people of the most widely differing cultures under heaven. It is true that his educational message needs to be studied at still greater depth, to be adapted and renewed with intelligence and courage, precisely because of changed social, cultural, ecclesial and pastoral contexts. It will be well to keep in mind the new lines of thought and the developments that have taken place in many fields, the signs of the times and the indications of Vatican II. Nevertheless the substance of his teaching remains intact; the unique nature of his spirit, his intuitions, his style, his charisma are unchanged, because they draw their inspiration from the transcendent pedagogy of God.[1]

Reflecting on the above words of Pope John Paul II, the seventh Superior General of the Salesians urged all members of the Salesian Family to go back to the *preventive system* and invited all to come up with a new *preventive system:* "We have to propose a *new preventive system.* Today we speak of *new* evangelization, *new* education; so it seems necessary also to speak of a *new* [all italics added] preventive system. This does not mean that we are to do away with what we have, but we have to invent a new way of understanding and applying it, with new emphases and new priorities. If up to the present we have been experts in the preventive system, so too we must become experts in the new preventive system."[2]

Hopefully this attempt to present the pastoral approach of St. John Bosco will fulfill the wish of our Superior General and that of all the followers and admirers of this great educator. We can apply what was said about other outstanding leaders to our own context: "We have been able to do so much because we were carried on the shoulders of great giants."

In his masterful letter "The Christian Education of Youth," Pope Pius XI wrote: "The true Christian, product of Christian education, is the supernatural man who thinks, judges, and acts constantly and consistently in accordance with right reason illumined by the supernatural light of the example and teaching of Christ; in other words, to use the current term, the true and finished man of character."[3]

This philosophy of education has become a permanent commitment of the Church, ever faithful to the mandate of Christ to teach all nations. In a special way the religious orders of men and women joined by countless dedicated lay persons have sought to implement this Catholic philosophy of education through a unique spirit or method inherited from their respective founders or foundresses. The special approach adopted and practiced by St. John Bosco and then bequeathed to his followers is called the *preventive system*. Over forty thousand priests, brothers, and sisters as well as countless lay persons throughout the world apply this method as they guide the young in an atmosphere of kindness, with the hope of forming true Christian men and women who will live according to right reason and the Gospel.

Don Bosco possessed a dynamic personality that attracted many, especially the young, for whom he always had a deep and kindly concern. Throughout his writings we find great insistence on the need for friendly relationships and personal contact if one is to have any influence on the young. He was able to establish a group of religious and lay collaborators, trained by him personally, to perpetuate his method of education, which was so well adapted to the psychology of the young. Don Bosco recognized the role of the laity. A hundred years before Vatican II, he established a Salesian Family that included not only priests, sisters, and brothers but also Salesian Cooperators—"Salesians without vows"—who carried out the Salesian mission according to their state in life and the needs of the local Church. Salesian alumni and alumnae, many of whom retain close ties with their former teachers, involve themselves in different facets of Salesian work.

Don Bosco not only had a profound insight into the minds of teenagers, but he was also keenly aware of the environment in which they were living. He knew that education stems from a particular culture and ought to be an instrument to better that culture. In his day society had a great influence on the impressionable minds of the young soon to be caught up in the throes of the Industrial Revolution and in the malaise of the political upheaval taking place in Italy. The center of this unrest was the city of Turin.

Realizing the power and importance of education, Don Bosco familiarized himself with the different theories of pedagogy then in practice. He discussed problems with the leading professors of the University of Turin and spent time visiting various outstanding schools. Provided with a wealth of theoretical educational knowledge and a keen sense of life's realities gained from his experience in working with youth, he launched a program of action well adapted to the physical, moral, psychological, and emotional needs of the young.

Don Bosco's method was a success then and still is today. The reason for this is that he was a man of God. Endowed by the

Lord with extraordinary powers and enriched with supernatural gifts, he used these blessings to prepare citizens for time and for eternity. Almighty God blessed his zeal and dedication with heavenly inspirations and even miracles. How else can we account for the rapid growth of the great Salesian Family founded by this "poor shepherd from Becchi," as he humbly called himself?

Don Bosco kept repeating, "Education is a matter of the heart." This book, *Keys to the Hearts of Youth,* is another effort to make known to the public Don Bosco's unique approach to youth as practiced today on five continents in the hope of reaching today's young, who are tomorrow's leaders. This Salesian approach to the hearts of adolescents stems from the Gospel of love. In the New Testament we hear Christ call the little ones to Himself: "Let the children come to me." He also left us the parable of the prodigal son, with its emphasis on the merciful father who awaits the return of the prodigal—it could have been a loving mother anxiously awaiting the return of a wayward daughter. Or again, when Jesus is invited to visit the dying daughter of Jairus, a leader of the synagogue, he restores her to life. And then there is the centurion's son. . . . So many moving scenes in the Gospel show us Christ's tenderness to the young.

Through the ages, philosophers and educators sought the key to the hearts of the young in order to prepare them for the responsible roles they had to play in society. Civil and religious leaders did not throw up their arms in despair. I think they rolled up their sleeves and accepted conditions as they were and tried to find solutions.

Chapter 1 highlights the problems of today's youth and presents one possible approach as practiced and developed by St. John Bosco (1815–1888). Reflecting on the early years of this nineteenth-century educator, we show how his ideas took root in the experiences of his own youth. He grew up in a single-parent family, guided by the strong character of his widowed mother,

Margaret. He learned to cope with the inevitable domestic tension that arose between him and his stepbrother Anthony, who vehemently opposed John's effort to acquire an education, so necessary if John were to become a priest in the service of youth. This period of his life will be detailed in Chapter 2.

Chapter 3 will describe the challenges that lay ahead when he began his life's mission. Establishing a permanent home and recruiting followers were two huge obstacles he had to confront and overcome. The sprawling city of Turin in northern Italy, a scene of political strife and wrenching social change, was a magnet for hordes of restless youths. Finding himself in the midst of this maelstrom, he put his shoulders to the wheel and advanced his method of education and rehabilitation. His success led him to establish two religious orders, one for men (1859) and the other for women (1872).

The questions you may be asking—Who is Don Bosco? Where is his place in the history of education?—will be answered in this book. Chapter 4 will place Don Bosco in the center of the nineteenth century as he began his work in 1841. After his death in 1888, his followers continued his mission, which today continues worldwide. In his own day he was personally acquainted with secular educators and their theories. The greatest influence, however, came from other religiously oriented men and women who followed the Gospel in presenting spiritual ideals while putting to good use the scientific data offered by different schools of education. These dedicated teachers looked after the whole person: physically, morally, socially, intellectually. Chapters 5, 6, and 7 present a complete picture of the total education given by Don Bosco. Like other religious educators, he strove to prepare the young to take their place in society and to contribute to it. It must be said, however, that his main emphasis was on moral and religious education. His phrase *good Christian and useful citizen* implied that the latter depended on the former.

What was so special about Don Bosco's approach? What made his method so attractive and successful? He based his system on three key words: reason, religion, and kindness; and these core values explain his success. Striving always to be reasonable in an atmosphere of gentleness while developing moral principles, he worked to shape a student's character and help him/her to find eternal salvation.

The concluding chapter summarizes the contribution that Don Bosco and his followers have made to society and to the Church. Three appendixes present seminal documents that articulate the philosophy and practice of his method. These writings contain insights that will inspire those dedicated to the formation and care of youth.

The author has made every effort to employ inclusive language, but he has not edited quotations from the nineteenth and early twentieth centuries to reflect the sensibilities of a later era. The reader must make some allowances, especially when studying the seminal documents appended to this book. One must also keep in mind that most of what is written in those documents refers to boarding schools. The underlying principles of reason, religion, and kindness apply to all contexts and circumstances, however, because they stem from the Gospel, which transcends time and place.

INTRODUCTION

1. Pope John Paul II, "*Juvenum Patris,*" in *Acts of the General Council of the Salesian Society of St. John Bosco,* no. 325 (New Rochelle, NY: Salesian Communications, 1988), 27.
2. Egidio Viganò, SDB, "Un Nuovo Sistema Preventivo," as quoted in the *Bollettino Salesiano* (Rome, Italy: Salesian Society, April 1995), 2.
3. Pope Pius XI, "The Christian Education of Youth," in *Seven Great Encyclicals* (Glen Rock, NJ: Paulist Press, 1963), 65.

1 Today's Youth, Tomorrow's Leaders

"Is There Really Hope in the Young?" That is the title of a chapter that begins on page 118 of the book, *Crossing the Threshold of Hope,* by His Holiness, John Paul II. In that book the Pope answered a series of questions regarding hope in and for the young.

"The very day of the inauguration of my papal ministry, October 22, 1978, at the conclusion of the Liturgy, I said to the young people gathered in St. Peter's Square: 'You are the hope of the Church and of the world. You are my hope.' I have often repeated these words."[1] The reporter queried the Holy Father: "The young people have a special place in the heart of the Holy Father who often repeats that the whole Church looks to them with particular hope for a new beginning of evangelization. Your Holiness, is this a realistic hope? Or are we adults only indulging in an illusion that each new generation will be better than ours and all those that came before?"[2]

The Holy Father answers by recalling his own experience as a young priest. He tells us that his most memorable insight was the discovery of youth. "During that time he searches, like the young man in the Gospel, for answers to basic questions; he searches not only for the meaning of life but also for a concrete way to go about living his life"[3] Pope John Paul is on target when he counsels parents and all youth leaders to always keep before them this focus of youth.

He cautions all youth counselors to respect the desire of the young to be their own persons and to find love. However, they need guides; and they want them to be close at hand. When the young turn to authority figures, they do so because they see in them a wealth of human warmth and a willingness to *walk* with them along the paths they are following.

Pope John Paul understands the hearts of the young. He possesses a special charisma in attracting youth from all over the world. The world youth rallies began in 1985 in Rome. He makes it clear that it is not he who brings the young from one end of the world to the other. "It is they who bring him! Even though he is getting older, they urge him to be young. They do not permit him to forget his experience, his discovery of youth, and its great importance for the life of every man. I believe this explains a great deal."[4] John Paul reveals his deep feeling when he says that "we need the enthusiasm of the young. We need their *joie de vivre*. In it is reflected some of the original joy God had in creating man. The young experience the same joy within themselves. The joy is the same everywhere, but it is also ever new and original."[5]

The Holy Father, ever conscious that he is the Vicar of Christ on earth, focuses the attention of the young always on Christ, "the way, the truth, and the life." He then goes on to speak of Christ and his bride, the Church: "It is also necessary that the young know the Church, that they perceive Christ in the Church, Christ who *walks* through the centuries alongside each generation, alongside every person. He *walks* alongside each person as a friend. An important day in a young person's life is the day in which he is convinced that Christ is the only Friend who will not disappoint him, on whom he can always depend."[6]

John Paul II is a prophet of hope when he speaks of the young. He goes out to meet them and to bolster their hope and enthusiasm. This is very evident in the Pope's regular visits to the parishes of Rome. Every visit must include a meeting with the young people. He desires to hear first of all what the young have to say to him. He finds in the young an immense potential for good and for creative possibility. Not only in Rome, but everywhere the Pope goes, he seeks out the young and the young seek him out. "Actually, in truth, it is not the Pope who is being sought out at all. The one being sought out is Christ, who knows 'that which is in every man' (John 2,25), especially in a young person, and who can give true answers to his questions!"[7]

Today's Reality

Realizing that John Paul is a prophet of hope and a beacon for the young, the reporter asked the Pope point-blank whether or not he was too optimistic about youth today. After all, the social situation is rather gloomy in regard to youth. The lives and the behavior of our young people today are influenced by many social forces: the breakdown of the family; a decline of trust in public officials due to corruption and questionable practices in government; and the impact of the mass media especially in regard to crime, violence, and sexual freedom.

Youth suffer a malaise because of low self-esteem, insecurity about the future, loneliness: all stemming from a sense of abandonment. The breakup of the family only makes more acute and painful the need for belonging, support, and love that we associate with the home. Strommen, in his research on youth, reports the cry of youth: "I want to be part of a family, where we all love, accept, and care for one another."[8]

Today's youth finds it difficult to make necessary decisions because of constant pressures and painful tensions that surround them: drugs, alcohol, sexual freedom, family problems, one-parent families, social prejudices, discrimination, gangs, violence in the streets and schools. This sad situation has spawned another major problem: that of adolescent suicide. According to the 1990 census, there are currently 4,000 to 5,000 suicides a year committed by young people. A recent survey by the National Conference of Catholic Bishops reports a deepening sense of hopelessness and despair among teenagers, with a pessimistic and bleak outlook for the future.[9]

Sad to say, in many areas schools are not of much help. Violence in the school halls is becoming only too common, with students carrying weapons into the buildings; so much so that many school systems have had to install metal detectors. Many parents' lack of interest compounds the problems confronting administrators, principals, and teachers. It is not uncommon for both parents to work, some holding two jobs, with the result that there is little communication between parent and child.

To the above factors one must add the decline in religious and moral values that has accompanied a growing commitment to secularism. The lack of role models has forced the young to find their own direction in a society that exalts freedom from restraint and that fails to inculcate personal responsibility and correct behavior. The young unfortunately fall victim to the imitation of false heroes presented to them through the media. Worst of all, the young have lost hope in the future and wallow in pessimism and despair, with no desire to make the efforts necessary to improve themselves and their society. Influenced by prophets of doom and gloom, the young feel that all is lost. Lack of motivation brings in its wake grief and anxiety, which replace joy and hope.

Present-day youth are exposed daily to hours of television that carry into the home scenes of military conflict, bloodshed, and violence coming from all over the world. Arms sales to third-world countries only serve to enkindle the fires of hatred and a desire for revenge and destruction. Likewise the pervasive use of drugs is destroying the younger generation. Shootings and killings for the control of drug turfs make for more pessimism and despair.

The above picture does not mean that there are no solutions. Things may and can get worse unless we all put our shoulders to the wheel and try to contribute to the rebuilding of society. It is not an impossible task! Other periods of history had their problems when all was thought to be lost. The prophets of doom and gloom were replaced by prophets of light and courage. These men and women all possessed the spark of love for humankind and would not give in to despair. Lay and religious leaders joined together with legislators and educators to help rebuild society.

Prophets of Hope

Our world has known many prophets of hope and optimism for the young like Pope John Paul II. The Holy Father himself singled out in 1988 a man who had a heart similar to his own. It did not make any difference that this individual had lived more than a century before him. We are speaking of St. John Bosco, whom the Pope proclaimed "Father and Teacher of Youth." For St. John Bosco, founder of a great spiritual family, one may say that the peculiar trait of his brilliance is linked with the educational method which he himself called the *preventive system*. In a certain sense this represents the quintessence of his pedagogical wisdom and constitutes the prophetic message which he has left to his followers and to the Church, and which has received attention from numerous educators and students of pedagogy.[10] St. John Bosco expressed his love for the young in these memorable words: "That you are young is enough to make me love you very much."[11] "I have promised God that I would give of myself to my last breath for my boys."[12]

The aim of this book is to single out one educator of the last century whose influence continues today in his followers throughout the world. His particular avenue of approach was effective in his own day and is still effective today. On the threshold of the twenty-first century, his followers are looking forward with courage, hope, and confidence in today's youth who will become tomorrow's leaders.

Advances in behavioral sciences and psychological research have confirmed many of Don Bosco's guidelines. His vision anticipated the approaches associated with today's educational theories and practices. "Don Bosco's techniques anticipated many of the principles used by educators today, which now appear, for the most part, to be taken for granted. A pedagogy which offers the young a sense of contentment, joy, and fulfillment, such as that which forms the basis of Salesian schools of St. John Bosco throughout the world, is not unlike some contemporary views of education."[13]

A Farsighted Educator

Who was this individual who was admired and followed by so many? His name is John Bosco (1815–1888). Over forty thousand men and women in over one hundred countries follow and practice his method, which is based on three key elements: reason, religion, kindness—also known as the Salesian pastoral and educational triangle. He called his method the *preventive system* of education. While not a system in the strict sense of the word, his approach was very effective then and is still valid today. This technique was given to his followers in the conviction that the youth of all times could be guided to help prepare a better world for tomorrow. This method is founded on pastoral charity and is characterized by a sense of family and joy. The ultimate goal of this approach was and is to produce *good Christians and useful citizens.*

The first dimension of Don Bosco's methodology focuses on the concept of reason—the ability to know and understand the human dynamics of the young and to be able to communicate and dialogue with them. This reasonable stance calls for an active and constant presence on the part of the educator, for a pleasant and unrestrained being together. Through a friendly presence, the young come to know that the educator is available as a friend, guide, and counselor.

This approach is not restricted to the school scene, but it is for all circumstances. It is not sufficient for teachers to be seen in classroom situations with students. They must find occasions to mingle with students in hallways, in the cafeteria, and at academic, social, athletic, cultural, and religious events. These informal contacts are opportunities for dedicated educators to know and influence students, while at the same time becoming acquainted with their value systems and their goals. These encounters are graced moments for instilling permanent values that are "caught rather than taught."

Approached in this way, education becomes a creative and meaningful enterprise. A healthy rapport ensues and becomes a dynamic and constructive force in teaching. John Bosco used to say that students must not only be loved; they must know that they are loved. This he did by making himself available and by taking a keen interest in all activities—studies, work, sports, student clubs, and so on.

Another element in the Salesian triangle is kindness, which should not be viewed as a weakness but as a sign of strength and self-control. This element is closely related to reason, which always implies "to be reasonable," especially when misbehavior arises from thoughtlessness. Usually a kind word will suffice to bring the errant one back to duty and responsibility. Kindness creates a persuasive atmosphere where self-expression is fostered and openness encouraged. This interpersonal relationship generates confidence between pupils and teachers, who in Don Bosco's words are like "dedicated parents," encouraging and praising at the proper moment.

The Salesian educator seeks through kindness to minimize the negative effects of any "generation gap" by fostering a balance between authority and permissiveness, by blending freedom with responsibility, by bringing together the old and the new. In a word, this method of education promotes humanism.

Kindness must permeate the environment of a Salesian center, whether it is a classroom, a club, a school, or an athletic field. Don Bosco aimed to model each of his centers on a true home. Therefore, the element of kindness finds its true expression in the family spirit that exists in truly Christian families, a spirit of joy, love, and peace. The foundation of this educational method is illuminated by the words of St. Paul: "Charity is patient and kind. . . . Love bears all things, hopes all things, endures all things." (1 Cor 13:4,7.)

In this educational philosophy, the elements of reason and kindness are held together and find their basis in moral and religious training—that is to say, religion, the belief in a Supreme Being and the practice of the Gospel in love and service to all. It is precisely during the perplexing and confusing period of adolescence that moral values and ethical training need to be part of education. Personal responsibility is to be taught and demanded.

The public today is asking for moral training and is seeking a way of restoring moral behavior in our nation's schools. The reason for this is apparent as one considers the evils pervading our society due to a misguided permissiveness. As long as we keep God out of our schools, we deprive our young people of a system of values that could help all of them to lead good lives and benefit society. However, we must say that today there is a gradual return to values and character building.

During Don Bosco's times, as in our own, there were many moral and social problems. Without neglecting the human need for encouragement and rapport, he put the emphasis where it belonged: on moral training and ethical behavior. He could not conceive of "amoral education." For John Bosco the three Rs could have no meaning without the presence of a fourth R—religion.

Speaking in 1855 to the Prime Minister of Italy, Urbano Rattazzi (1808–1873), Don Bosco outlined his program. "In the application of this method, care is taken to instill respect for God in the hearts of the young, through suitable instruction. They are encouraged to do good and to avoid evil through an enlightened conscience sustained by religion." (*Biographical Memoirs,* Vol. 5, pp. 36–37.)

Years before, in our country, George Washington struck the same note on the need for morality. In his "Farewell Address" he said: "Let us with caution indulge the supposition that morality can be maintained without religion. Whatever can be conceded to the influence of refined education on minds of peculiar structure, reason and experience forbid us to expect that national morality can prevail to the exclusion of religious principle."[14]

I would like to conclude this chapter with the story of a modern hero. His name is Sean Devereux. This young Briton was educated by the followers of St. John Bosco. After graduation, he taught in a Salesian school in England. A number of years later, he followed his teachers to the mission fields of Liberia, Africa. He then joined the United Nations relief effort in Somalia where he met his death helping the poor children of Somalia.

The Bridge over the River Juba

The title may remind you of the movie *The Bridge over the River Kwai,* but the place and the hero are different. The rebuilt bridge in Somalia is now named after a Salesian graduate from England who was shot to death on January 2, 1993. He was delivering aid to the starving children in the gun-scarred port city of Kismayu in Somalia. Sean Devereux was only twenty-eight when he was murdered. He had already spent five years working for UNICEF, the United Nations International Children's Emergency Fund.

Sean's father, Dermot, remembers his son saying: "While my heart beats, I have to do what I think I can; that is, help those who are less fortunate." In a letter sent to Mr. and Mrs. Devereux, the UN Secretary General, Dr. Boutros-Boutros Ghali, said: "In adverse and often dangerous circumstances Sean showed complete dedication to his work. His colleagues admired his energy, his courage, and his compassion. Sean was an exemplary staff member and gave his life serving others."

Sean pursued his secondary education at the Salesian School in Farnborough, southeast of London. It was in this caring and familial environment that he developed endearing traits of ready friendship, firm leadership, and organizational ability. These qualities, anchored in his moral character, led to his appointment as a student leader. During these adolescent years he matured into a fine gentleman, combining good humor, constant efficiency, and generous service.

After majoring in physical education and geography at Birmingham University, he began teaching at the Salesian School in Chertsey, a village of gardens and flowers on the Thames less than twenty miles from London. After three happy years of successful teaching (and coaching winning teams of rugby and cricket), his ideals called him elsewhere. He committed himself to follow in the footsteps of St. John Bosco, caring for youth. As a student and as a teacher in Salesian schools, he was imbued with the *reason, religion, kindness,* educational theory of this saint. It was natural for him then to ask to work with the British Salesians who were working in Liberia. His offer was accepted. One of Sean's teachers stated at his funeral: "All his fine qualities seemed to blossom more than ever. By this time I was in Liberia myself and was able to see the relationship he had built up with the Liberian boys and girls."

He was assigned to the Salesian School in Tappita. In 1990, civil war broke out and forced the closing of all schools. Whole peoples were being massacred; food supplies were cut off; homes and shops were destroyed. This sad state of affairs touched Sean's heart—especially the unfortunate state of young boys and girls, who had all endeared themselves to him. He decided to join the UN refugee program. As the fighting reached its height, Sean and other relief workers were ordered out of the country. UNICEF invited him to work in the neighboring country of Sierra Leone. From there Sean was sent to Somalia, where he went with optimism and generosity.

In Somalia UNICEF assigned him to organize relief for the starving, with a focus on children—much to Sean's delight. His base of operations was Kismayu, the stronghold of one of the many warlords who had torn the country apart. It was here that Sean was to meet his death while carrying supplies for the poor and needy, trying to bring relief and hope in the ravages of war, death, and pestilence.

Sean lived by hope, especially hope for the young. On November 15, 1992, he wrote in a letter to his parents: "Next to the football [soccer] field, there is an open area with hundreds of earth mounds. These are the graves of boys and girls who died about six months ago! The contrast is so stark! But as I watched the energy and laughter of the children as they kicked the ball, it brought home to me the message that where there is life there is always hope."

Chapters 2 and 3 will introduce the person who is the reason for our book, St. John Bosco, whom Sean and so many others learned to love and imitate in his love for the young, in the hope of building a better world for the future.

CHAPTER 1

1. Pope John Paul II, *Crossing the Threshold of Hope* (New York: Alfred A. Knopf, 1994), 125.
2. Ibid., 118.
3. Ibid., 121.
4. Ibid., 125.
5. Ibid.
6. Ibid., 126.
7. Ibid., 123–124.
8. M. P. Strommen, *Five Cries of Youth* (San Francisco: Harper and Row, 1988), 42.
9. Paul K. Henderson, "Pastoral Needs of Youth," in *Network Papers,* no. 24 (New Rochelle, NY: Don Bosco Multimedia, 1989), 1–3.

10. Pope John Paul II, "*Juvenum Patris,*" Rome, Italy, 1988, no. 8.
11. Giovanni Bosco, *Il Giovane Proveduto* (Turin, Italy: Salesian Society, 1847), 7. Quoted by the Holy Father, ibid., no. 4.
12. Eugenio Ceria, *Memorie Biografiche di S. Giovanni Bosco,* vol. 18 (Turin, Italy: Società Editrice Internazionale, 1937), 258. Quoted by the Holy Father, ibid., no. 4.
13. S. Mary Mullaly, FMA, "A Study of the Viability of the Preventive System of St. John Bosco for the Youth of Today in Salesian Sisters' Schools" (Ed. D. diss., University of San Francisco, 1990), 74.
14. Henry Steele Commager, ed., *Documents of American History* (New York: F. S. Craft and Co., 1946), 173.

2 A Man Sent by God Whose Name Was John

One of the titles that Pope John Paul II has given John Bosco is "Father and Teacher of Youth." It is remarkable that John Bosco came to stand as a father to so many, for his own father passed away when he was only two years old. The words uttered then by his mother, Mamma Margaret, remained deeply impressed on his mind, "My poor son, come with me. You no longer have a father."[1] This loss seems to have led him to seek out father figures, especially in the early part of his life. One such person was Fr. John Calosso (1760–1830), a retired priest who took a personal interest in John and helped further his elementary studies and his Christian formation. When Fr. Calosso died, John wept. Later, John would write in his memoirs: "I have always prayed for this outstanding benefactor of mine and I shall continue to do so for the rest of my life. . . . It was then that I came to realize what it was to have a regular spiritual director, a faithful friend of one's soul. . . . He taught me how to make a short daily meditation, or more accurately, a spiritual reading. From then on I began to savor the spiritual life."[2] John in time would become a master spiritual director for the young.

Educational Awakenings

Though John felt the loss of his father keenly, this early misfortune did not make him an anxious or timid child. He developed a warm, deep, and affectionate relationship with Mamma Margaret. The "mothering one" (to use an expression of the American psychiatrist, Harry Stack Sullivan) took special care of this tender plant that would in time become an enormous tree that sheltered many. She encouraged, affirmed, and guided John, who trusted her always. This rapport did not destroy his unconscious need to establish a father-son relationship. That need would soon be fulfilled by his becoming a surrogate father to many other young people. From his earliest years, John showed an earnest desire to do good to his friends, and he began to exercise a moral influence over them—even those who were older and bigger. He was drawn to gather children around himself and teach them catechism (the price of attendance at his magic and acrobatic shows). As he himself said, it seemed to him that this was the only thing he had to do on earth. Were these early indications of what the future held in store?

Mamma Margaret scolded John when he would come home bruised and bleeding from these sessions in which he had enlivened the catechism with his own acrobatics. She relented when he would explain that in his presence, the boys behaved themselves and refrained from using bad language. John seems to have realized early that young people need a gentle and affable friend. John himself often unburdened himself to his mother, who always gave an attentive ear.

Yet she often could not fathom him, especially when he complained that the parish priest was unapproachable. Hoping to establish something like the close relationship he had enjoyed with Fr. John Calosso, the boy often arranged to run into the pastor out walking with his assistant. The priests would return his greeting courteously and continue on their way. The pastor never uttered a friendly word to win his heart or inspire confidence.

One day John complained to his mother about this apparent indifference. She explained that the priest was a busy man. John was not satisfied and told his mother that if he ever became a priest, he would act differently. "I would look for boys and get them around me. I would want them to know that I care for them and desire their friendship. I would speak kindly to them, and give good advice and dedicate myself to their spiritual welfare.

How I would love to have a chance to talk with my pastor, just as I did with Father John Calosso. Why shouldn't it be so?"[3]

The Dream

At an early age John was eager to be of help to his peers and to teach them right from wrong. This desire and zeal were abetted by a vision. John called it a dream. He was nine years old when he had this prophetic dream. At the command of the Holy Father, Pius IX, John recounted the dream:

> At the age of nine I had a dream which remained deeply impressed upon my mind for the rest of my life. In a dream I seemed to be near a house in a large courtyard, where a crowd of boys was gathered together. Some were laughing, others playing, and many among them blaspheming. On hearing these blasphemies, I immediately rushed into their midst, raising my voice and using my fists to make them quiet.
>
> At that moment a dignified looking man, nobly clad, who seemed to be in the prime of life, appeared on the scene. A white mantle covered the whole of his person, but his face was so radiant that I was unable to look at it for long. He called me by name, and directed me to place myself at the head of these boys, concluding with these words: "You must win the hearts of these friends of yours, not with violence but with sweetness and charity. Set to work at once to instruct them on the wickedness of vice and on the excellence of virtue."
>
> The vision continued. The grand personage was Christ, the Good Shepherd. Later our Lady appeared, took me by the hand, and said: "Look." Glancing around I realized that the youngsters had all apparently run away. A large number of goats, dogs, cats, bears, and other animals took their place. She then said: "This is the field of your labor. Make yourself humble, determined, and strong. You must do for my sons what you will now see happen to these animals."
>
> I looked again, and to my surprise, instead of fierce animals, I now saw gentle lambs, all frisking about and bleating merrily,

as if to do honor to the MAN and WOMAN. At this point of the dream I commenced to cry and begged the Lady to speak clearly because I did not know what all these things meant. She then put her hand on my head and said: "In good time, my son, you will understand everything."[4]

John wasted no time in telling his family about this dream; he spoke to his brothers, his grandmother, and his mother. Each had a different interpretation. His brother Joseph said: "You're going to become a keeper of sheep and goats." His half-brother Anthony merely grunted, "Perhaps you might become a gang leader." His grandmother, with the wisdom of age, remarked that we should pay no attention to dreams. Mamma Margaret, who knew John well, simply said: "Who knows, you may become a priest." John was very pleased with this answer. It was to her that he had confided his ambition to care for many young people as a priest someday. How many hurdles were still to be overcome before he would attain that goal!

Schooling to Become a Priest

In the prophetic dream of 1824 it was made clear to John Bosco that study was indispensable if he was to fulfill his mission on behalf of the young. But John was having so much trouble obtaining an education that this command seemed an impossible dream. When he asked how it could be accomplished, the answer came at once: "I will give you a teacher. Under her guidance you can become wise. Without her all wisdom is foolishness."[5] The woman of the dream was Mary, who would make possible not only the acquisition of knowledge but also the fulfillment of his mission.

Mamma Margaret, aware of John's desire to become a priest, tried to help. John's studies, up to this point, had been most irregular. Better schooling was available in the nearby town of Castelnuovo. This choice would entail heavy expenses, and there was strong opposition from her stepson Anthony, the main breadwinner. Whenever the subject of study came up, there was tension. Fearing that something might happen between Anthony and John, since neither would compromise, Margaret came to a painful decision. John was sent to work as a farmhand with some friends, the Moglias, where he stayed for two years (February 1827–November 1, 1829). He was now fourteen years of age. Through the intervention of his uncle Michael, John returned home. During this time, Mamma Margaret had set things in motion for the division of the property. Anthony was now of age and could go off on his own.

Fr. John Calosso's interest in John dates back to this time. Fr. Calosso was impressed by the boy's intelligence and even more by his eagerness to study in the hope of becoming a priest. He undertook to help John with his studies and introduced him to the world of grammar and composition. The good priest went beyond that and became his spiritual director. John states that he began to appreciate the spiritual life through his direction, spiritual reading, and meditation.

This happiness did not last long. Father Calosso died suddenly on November 21, 1830. John's world collapsed. The good priest had left a sizable sum of money for John's education; rather than get involved in inheritance squabbles with Fr. Calosso's family, however, John renounced the bequest. He was badly shaken. "Fr. Calosso's death was a great loss to me. I wept inconsolably over my dead benefactor. I thought of him in my waking hours and dreamt of him when I was asleep. It affected me so badly that my mother feared for my health. She sent me for a while to my grandfather." In Father Calosso, John had found a substitute father; and at his passing, he must have remembered the words his mother had spoken to him when he was two years old, "You no longer have a father!" I emphasize this episode that we may better understand the keen loss John felt and how this experience prepared him to become the

"Father and Teacher of Youth," as Pope John Paul II has named him. At this time, John Bosco was favored with another spiritual dream, in which he was chided for putting his trust in men rather than in our heavenly Father.[6]

Leaving Home

The decision was made to have John complete his elementary studies at Castelnuovo, three miles distant from his native village of Becchi. At first he went back and forth twice a day, a trek of twelve miles. This was too much. His mother boarded him in Castelnuovo with a tailor named John Roberto. This move, and others to come, were providential. It was from this man that John learned tailoring. In addition, Mr. Roberto played the violin and the organ. John, being a quick and eager student, learned to play both instruments, and these skills would serve him well later in his ministry.

After about a year in this small town, John had completed his elementary education; and it was time for him to move on to Chieri, where a course of study on the secondary and junior college levels was available. Education was more expensive now; more sacrifices had to be borne by Mamma Margaret and friends, and John had to learn the difficult art of begging, which would play a role in the development of his educational mission.

He spent ten years at Chieri, six of them in the seminary. During this decade (1831–1841), John had to work to pay for his schooling. For the first two years he boarded with Mrs. Lucy Matta, whose son he tutored in partial payment of his board. The remaining two years he worked for a café owner, as well as for a blacksmith, a shoemaker, and a carpenter. Later on, his familiarity with these trades would help him establish vocational schools. In time, Don Bosco's followers would establish technical schools the world over.

A Teenage Leader

John's mother, affectionately known by the boys and early Salesians as Mamma Margaret, gave her son a Christian education early in life. It was to be this way till the end of her earthly life. She spent the last decade of her life with John as his apostolate began to unfold. She was a brave woman, wise and prudent. Mamma Margaret passed on to her children the gospel she lived and practiced. Her son Joseph became the father of a good family and continued his life as a farmer. Her stepson Anthony, the cause of so much heartache, eventually found his way in life and made peace with Mamma Margaret and John. She believed that moral principles and Christian behavior were the foundation of a peaceful and successful life. Although she had been raised in dire poverty and had to raise her own family in conditions not much better, her faith in God was never shaken.

At this important period of his life, the teachings and encouragement of his saintly mother were to help John meet the challenge of finding his own way in the world. A noted biographer of John Bosco, Fr. Eugenio Ceria, emphasizes the adjustments that this young man had to make.

In need of formal education, John was forced to leave the safety and tranquillity of country life and enter the dangerous and tempting life of the city, with its new experiences and uncertain friends. John, in full adolescence, had to choose his company carefully. He chose a priest as his confessor and counselor. The zealous priest, while offering wise counsels, recommended a life of prayer and devout reception of the sacraments. The following are John's words: "I am greatly indebted to this priest if I did not fall victim to evil and get led into serious problems."[7]

In his personal memoirs, John stated that some students wanted him to gamble for money. More than one tried to make him his partner in vandalizing expeditions; and one of them once dared to suggest that he should steal his landlady's money.

Such encounters brought John to the realization that with certain teenagers he could do nothing. He was also aware that with the majority he could play an important role and lead them to follow a secure path.

An original idea struck him one day, as he pondered ways to fulfill his desire to be an apostle—a desire that was with him constantly. At seventeen years of age (1832), John organized a group of young people, and he named this group "The Merry Company" (La Società dell'Allegria). This association was one of authentic Christian fellowship. There were only two rules: all members had to avoid bad language and attend seriously to their Christian and scholastic duties. Further, each one was to combat sadness and gloom. Joy and optimism were later to be essential elements of St. John Bosco's educational method. Under John's leadership, this group roamed the hills, played a variety of games, listened to good readings.

The parents of these youngsters were delighted, especially when they saw the results: progress in study, fidelity to house chores, and respect for the neighbors. On occasion, John would put on a show with his magic tricks and expert juggling, culminating in prayers and a recounting of the Sunday sermon, which John could repeat almost word for word. "As in former days, all honest and keen merriment ended with prayer; the group had its own meetings; all sorts of discussions would take place; religious topics were lively and frank. On Sundays John would lead the group to the Jesuit church for the afternoon religious instruction, crammed with stories and examples given by the good Fathers to the eager listeners." (Cf. Auffray, p. 52.)

The Influence of a Mother

In today's world, too many young people have reason to feel abandoned by their parents. Some are raised by elderly grandparents; some become parents themselves in their teens. Under these circumstances, there is a deep loss of personal worth and a lowering of self-esteem. Not finding the care and love they need at home, the young will seek out groups that give them a feeling of belonging and self-worth. Today, gangs are prevalent; some are organized even in the elementary grades. This situation can lead to destructive and corrupting experiences. There are, however, many public and private agencies that seek to provide a warm environment and a substitute for the experience of a family. These organizations do much to build character by providing for growth in self-esteem and personal worth. (Cf. Strommen, 1988, p. 68.)

There is no doubt that in the normal home environment, the mother plays a crucial role not only in the physical growth of her child, but also in his or her emotional and psychic development. With the premature death of her husband, Margaret remained faithful to her vocation of motherhood and raised her three children with care, love, and vigilance. Though she was illiterate, her life and example gave her children much to learn from. This one-parent home was functional. In most one-parent families today, the parent (usually a mother) must work outside the home for many hours each day, an arrangement under which it is hard for the home to remain functional.

One of John Bosco's biographers, Fr. Giovanni Lemoyne, was of the opinion that "John modeled himself on his mother."[8] He was to exhibit the same faith, the same purity, the same love of prayer. From her he learned patience, fearlessness, constancy, trust in God, zeal for the spiritual good of one's neighbor, simplicity and gentleness of manner, and charity for all. John was also to learn her prudence in managing affairs, her careful supervision of those under her charge, and her serenity in the face of adversity.

The Seminary

In the fall of 1835, John entered the seminary to begin the final stage on his road to the priesthood. He was twenty years old. The night before, Mamma Margaret spoke to John as only a mother would: "When you came into the world, I consecrated you to the Blessed Virgin; when you began your schooling, I recommended you exclusively to the Madonna. Now I beg you to belong to her entirely. Love those who love her, and if someday you become a priest, constantly promote devotion to this good Mother." Margaret and John both began to cry. He broke the silence: "Mother, before leaving you for my new life, let me thank you for all you have done for me. Your counsels are engraved upon my soul, and they will be my treasure from which I shall draw every day."[9] Later in this book we shall dwell at length on the role that Mary, the Lady of his prophetic dream, played in the life of John Bosco.

The seminary course lasted seven years. Because of John's maturity and intelligence, the Archbishop of Turin allowed him to omit the sixth year and just sit for the exams. During these intense years of preparation, John still had to help pay for his board and tuition expenses. Rendering services to his fellow seminarians, winning financial prizes for scholarship each year, serving as a sacristan—by these means as well as the aid of his spiritual director Fr. Joseph Cafasso (now a canonized saint), he paid his expenses.

John did not neglect his friends. Each Thursday afternoon the seminarians were free; and John would spend this time relaxing with his young friends, playing games with them, counseling and encouraging. For John, "this was the highlight of the week."[10] Even during the summer months his delight was to be with the young. One of his seminary classmates recalled him in those early days: "He loved them, instinctively, because he was grieved at their neglect; he loved them as a matter of vocation, because he knew that he was called to serve them."[11]

In Turin, on June 5, 1841, he was ordained a priest by Archbishop Aloysius Franzoni, who was to be John Bosco's friend, admirer, and supporter in his mission to the poor youth.

Turin would soon become his field of apostolic work. It was in this city that he would lay the foundation of his worldwide mission on behalf of youth. From this day on, John was called Don Bosco (the word *Don* is a respectful title used in Italian to address a priest by name). Because of his popularity in all corners of the globe, the title has become familiar to millions who do not speak Italian.

The joy of Mamma Margaret was beyond all description. Her years of pain and sacrifice could not be compared to the happiness of this day. When John returned home for his First Mass and celebration, his thoughts went back to his years of struggle and anxiety; above all his heart was full of emotion, especially when he was alone with his mother, after all the excitement of the day. As Mamma Margaret took his consecrated hands in her own calloused peasant hands she said: "You are now a priest, and you celebrate Mass. You are, therefore, closer to Jesus Christ. But remember that to begin to say Mass is to begin to suffer. You will not become aware of this immediately, but little by little you will realize that your mother was right. I am sure that you will pray for me every day, whether I be still living or dead, and that is enough for me. From now on you must think only of saving souls; never worry about me."[12]

The influence of Mamma Margaret would continue till her death in 1856. The last decade of her life was to be spent at the side of her son in the city of Turin, where she would also be a mother to the first youngsters who came to live at the Oratory.

On February 8, 1995, in the Basilica of Mary, Help of Christians, commenced the official process for the beatification and canonization of Mamma Margaret. This event took place at Valdocco, where nearly one hundred fifty years earlier (April 12, 1846) Don Bosco had taken possession of the shed where his worldwide mission began. On November 3, 1846, Mamma Margaret came to live with her son in those few rented rooms. For ten years she generously collaborated with him and stood by him. Only he knew how much it cost his mother to leave Becchi and come to the city of Turin. We members of the Salesian Family acknowledge her contribution to the success, the style, the familial atmosphere, and the spirit of kindness and sacrifice that still continue to characterize all of Don Bosco's institutions throughout the world.

CHAPTER 2

1. John Bosco, *Memoirs of the Oratory of St. Francis de Sales from 1811–1855,* trans. Daniel Lyons, SDB, with notes and commentary by Eugenio Ceria, SDB, Lawrence Castelvecchi, SDB, and Michael Mendl, SDB (New Rochelle, NY: Don Bosco Publications, 1989), 8.
2. Ibid., 36.
3. Giovanni Battista Lemoyne, SDB, *The Biographical Memoirs of Saint John Bosco,* vol. 1, 1815–1840, an American edition translated from the original Italian, ed. Diego Borgatello, SDB (New Rochelle, NY: Salesiana Publishers, Inc., 1955), 170.
4. Paul Avallone, SDB, *Reason, Religion, Kindness—the Educational Method of St. John Bosco,* 3rd ed. (New Rochelle, NY: Don Bosco Publications, 1977), 61–62.
5. Bosco, *Memoirs,* 18.
6. Ibid., 48.
7. Eugenio Ceria, *Don Bosco Con Dio* (Rome, Italy: Direzione Generale, Opere Don Bosco, 1988), 47.
8. Lemoyne, *Biographical Memoirs,* 31.
9. A. Auffray, SDB, *Saint John Bosco* (Tirupattur, India: Salesian House, 1930), 52.
10. William R. Ainsworth, *Saint John Bosco, the Priest, the Man, the Times* (Bolton, England: Salesian Publications, n.d.), 31.
11. Auffray, *Saint John Bosco,* 61.
12. Bosco, *Memoirs,* 171.

3 The Early Apostolate

In November 1841, Don Bosco came to Turin, a large industrial city in northern Italy. The prophetic dream of 1824 was beginning to unfold as he found himself among the poor and abandoned youth at risk. Don Bosco had been encouraged by his spiritual director, Fr. Joseph Cafasso, to come to Turin for further training at the Convitto, a residence for young priests who desired further theological studies and pastoral practice in preaching, administering the sacraments, and giving religious instruction. Of the influence Fr. Cafasso had on his priestly formation, Don Bosco later said, "Fr. Cafasso, who for six years was my guide, was especially my spiritual director. If I have been able to do any good, I owe it to this worthy priest in whose hands I placed every decision I made, all my study, and every activity of my life."[1]

Don Bosco was to stay at the Convitto for three years (1841–1844); his ministry during this period included visits to the sick and the poor as well as to prisoners. This period of his life was pivotal; his great desire to care for youth grew stronger when he saw the misery and neglect of so many young people migrating to the city in search of a livelihood.

Although the Industrial Revolution had already taken hold in other countries of Europe, it was just beginning to make its appearance in northern Italy. Turin was the hub of this new development. At the same time, the Italian peninsula was undergoing political upheaval. In 1848 a liberal Constitution was adopted in the kingdom of Sardinia, which also comprised Piedmont and Savoy. This event marked the beginning of the *Risorgimento*—a political movement that led to the unification of Italy. The center of this movement was Turin. During this turmoil, Don Bosco stayed clear of politics and made his contribution by caring for the hordes of youths who had to come to the city. Some of these young migrants found employment as laborers, apprentices, masons, carpenters, and weavers; but many found no work and ended up homeless on the streets of Turin. In that era, society provided no "safety net."

Industrialization drew young people from the countryside into the burgeoning cities. Those who were fortunate enough to find jobs as workers or service boys often had to work long hours in dangerous and inhumane conditions. The factory workers, both men and boys, put in fifteen hours a day or more, depending on the length of daylight. Don Bosco came upon a world of immature juveniles often abandoned by their parents and reduced to begging or surviving by other means, not always the best. Many of them landed in one of Turin's four prisons. It was with these unfortunates that the young and inexperienced Don Bosco began his social and Christian work. This experience was to be both formative and painful, as it opened his eyes to terrible social conditions and led him to seek ways to remedy them. His mission was beginning to unfold.

Encouraged by his mentor, Fr. Joseph Cafasso, Don Bosco began to visit prisons and houses of detention. He came across a great number of boys, ranging in age from twelve to eighteen who appeared healthy, strong, and intelligent. He was distressed to see them idle and listless all day long. During these visits he came to realize that those unfortunate youths could have been saved, if only a kind and interested person had offered a helping hand. Don Bosco left his own reflections in writing:

> I saw large numbers of young lads aged from 12 to 18, fine healthy youngsters, alert of mind, but seeing them idle there, infested with lice, lacking food for body and soul, horrified me.... What shocked me most was to see that many of them were released full of good resolutions to go straight, and yet in a short time they landed back in prison within a few days of their release.... I thought to myself, "if these youngsters had a friend

outside who would help them, take care of them, teach them religion on feast days. . . . Who knows but they could be steered away from ruin, or at least the number of those who return to prison could be lessened."[2]

It was only in 1855 that a juvenile correctional institution, the *Generala,* was opened. Don Bosco was a frequent visitor. Many came to visit him upon their release and Don Bosco helped them find jobs.

Laying the Foundations

The Feast of the Immaculate Conception, December 8, 1841, was a cold and dreary day! Don Bosco was vesting for Mass that morning when he heard a noise behind him. He turned to see a scuffle between the sacristan and a burly lad whom the sacristan was roughing up in the hope of persuading him to serve Don Bosco's Mass. The teenager protested that he did not know how. He had only come into the sacristy to get away from the cold outside. The sacristan gave the boy a cuff on the ear and chased him out. For a moment Don Bosco was caught off guard, and then suddenly ordered the man to go out and call the boy back. At the same time he told the sacristan that what he did was no way to treat his friend. Thinking to himself what kind of friends Don Bosco had and fearing for his job, the sacristan returned shortly with the trembling boy. When the youth timidly approached, Don Bosco assured him: "Come here my friend. . . . I will do you no harm. What is your name?"

"Bartholomew Garelli."

"Where do you come from?"

"Asti."

"What are you?"

"A mason."

"Are your parents alive?"

"No, both dead."

"How old are you?"

"Sixteen."

"Can you read and write?"

"No."

"Sing or whistle?"

The boy began laughing: the ice was broken; friendship was born.

"Tell me, Bartholomew: have you made your first Communion?"

"Not yet."

"Have you ever been to confession?"

"Yes, long ago, when I was a child."

"Do you say your prayers?"

"I have forgotten them."

"Do you go to Mass on Sundays?"

"Oh yes, almost always."

"Do you go to catechism?"

"I don't dare to."

"Why?"

"For shame. Smaller boys than me know more about it."

"Well, if I explained the catechism to you would you come?"

"I'd be very glad to."

"When shall we begin?"

"When you like."

"This evening?"

"Yes."

"And why not now?"

"If you like."

When Don Bosco finished celebrating Mass, he took Bartholomew aside and began to instruct him. He began with the Sign of the Cross. When this first short lesson was over, Don Bosco said:

"You will come back, won't you?"

"I will, indeed," said the lad.

"Then don't come alone. Bring your pals with you."[3]

The following Sunday, Bartholomew came with six other boys, all more ignorant than himself in matters of the catechism but wise in the ways of the street. Don Bosco received them all with a father's concern and love; he then began caring for them, finding them jobs, and guiding them in leading a good life. This first gathering was the seed that would grow into a big tree under whose shade thousands and thousands would find love and security as they learned to become "good Christians and useful citizens."

The Wandering Oratory (1844–1846)

The word "oratory" was in use since the time of St. Philip Neri (1515–1595) and St. Charles Borromeo (1538–1584) in the cities of Rome and Milan, respectively. The term designated a place of prayer, recreation, reading, and religious instruction. The environment offered a haven from the rough side of life; at the same time, guidance and counseling were always available. In Don Bosco's time, Turin and other cities of Italy enjoyed the benefits of oratories run by zealous lay men and lay women as well as by priests. However, the word gradually came to be associated with Don Bosco and his followers. On December 8, 1844, the Marchioness Barolo, a generous and social-minded citizen of Turin, allowed Don Bosco to use a large empty space in one of her unfinished hospitals. To these temporary quarters he gave the name "The Oratory of St. Francis de Sales," the same title would later designate the first permanent foundation at Valdocco on Easter Sunday 1846. Valdocco became the model of all Salesian centers throughout the world. The Constitutions of the Salesians give us a descriptive definition: "Don Bosco lived a pastoral experience in his first Oratory which serves as a model; it was for the youngsters a home that welcomed, a parish that evangelized, a school that prepared them for life, and a play-ground where friends could meet and enjoy themselves."[4]

On the third Sunday of October 1844, Don Bosco left the Convitto and became chaplain to one of Marchioness Barolo's institutions for girls. He could not receive in his small living quarters the large number of boys who now looked to him for guidance and encouragement. So there came into being, for a year and a half, an oratory "on the move." For the weekly gathering, Don Bosco took his group into the country. He organized games and the boys enjoyed themselves immensely. In this work Don Bosco was assisted by his generous and faithful friend, Fr. John Borel. Don Bosco made himself available for confessions. The celebration of the Liturgy followed, with full participation in song and prayer. The afternoons were free; toward evening, the boys gathered for prayers, after which Don Bosco gave a short talk preparing them for Monday's workday and the struggles of the week. With promises that he would come around to visit them on their jobs, Don Bosco would dismiss them after announcing the time and place for next week's assembly. Before returning home, the older boys accompanied their father and guide to his quarters where Don Bosco enjoyed a well earned night's rest.

The assembly of many young men in shifting locations aroused suspicion in the political climate of that time. The police, fearing some kind of protest and revolt, kept a close eye on Don Bosco and his innovative activities. Complaints from alarmed citizens reached the city officials. It was becoming more difficult to find a meeting place. Landowners began revoking their permissions, as did the Filippi brothers who had kindly allowed the use of their fields. Don Bosco had to relocate to six different places before obtaining a permanent site.

It was Palm Sunday in 1846. Don Bosco was not his usual self and the older boys knew why. This was the last day they would gather on this turf. Don Bosco had been served notice not to return. Discouraged and saddened, as evening approached, he withdrew from the boys and began to sob. After five years of effort and pain he was now beginning to see the fruit of his work. This could be the end! Early in life, John had learned from Mamma Margaret that trust and faith in God would see him through all difficulties. At this juncture, the Father in heaven would indeed provide an answer, but only after bitter tears were shed. Hope was beginning to wane. Don Bosco left the following description of this dark moment: "I said nothing at all, but everybody knew how troubled and worried I was. On that evening as I ran my eyes over the crowd of children playing, I thought of the rich harvest awaiting my priestly ministry. With no one to help me, my energy gone, my health undermined, with no idea where I could gather my boys in the future, I was very disturbed. I withdrew to one side, and as I walked alone, I began to cry, perhaps for the first time. As I walked, I looked up to heaven and cried out, 'My God, why don't you show me where you want me to gather these children? Oh, let me know! Oh, show me what I must do!'"[5]

No sooner had Don Bosco made this prayer than a stranger approached him. This man had a message from his employer, who knew about Don Bosco's plight and wanted to sell him a parcel of land with a shed. Don Bosco could hardly believe his ears. Was this an answer to his prayers? Following the man a short distance, Don Bosco saw a dilapidated old shed at the end of a small field. Don Bosco hesitated, because the roof was so low. The man told him not to worry about the low ceiling. He could have a few feet dug away for more standing room. Don Bosco seized the opportunity and, although he could not afford the land, took out a lease on it.

With a heart full of gratitude, he returned to his anxious band of boys. What a roar of applause when they heard that now they had a permanent home to replace the Wandering Oratory. They would meet in the Valdocco district at the Pinardi field on the following Sunday—Easter! He and his boys would be celebrating Resurrection Day in their new home, which would eventually become the Motherhouse and center of the worldwide Salesian Mission. The little seed did become the sturdy tree, whose shade today covers more than one square block, with a grand Basilica, schools, shops, a theater, and playgrounds. How magnificent was the Lord with Don Bosco, who had seen all this in his dreams.

The anxieties and frustrations of the first five years (1841–1846) took their toll. After the establishment of Don Bosco's first Oratory in Valdocco, the poorest section of Turin, his health gave out and the doctors feared for his life. His boys became anxious about this generous and zealous priest. Some went so far as to ask God to take their lives in exchange for the life of Don Bosco. In June of that year, Don Bosco was forced to return home to Becchi for a long convalescence. Under the vigilant eyes of Mamma Margaret, he gradually regained his health. During this absence, Fr. Borel and other priest friends looked after the Oratory.

A Permanent Home

With the arrival of autumn, it was time for Don Bosco to return to Turin and pick up where he had left off. His boys were expecting him. There was still a rather serious problem which had to be solved before his return. Very close to the property which he purchased and to the house where he planned to live, there was a tavern with a place of ill repute attached to it. Don Bosco feared that he would become grist for the gossip mill if he were to live alone. No priest could live there without arousing suspicion. John consulted the pastor of his home parish, Fr. Cinzano—a trusted and loyal friend. The wise priest, knowing the caliber of Mamma Margaret, suggested that he take his mother along with him. John had thought about it but hesitated. Margaret was no longer young. After so many years of toil and labor she deserved to live out her remaining years in the peace and quiet of the country. In Turin there certainly would be no such luxury, with over three hundred lively boys surrounding her son. Finally, one day, John approached his mother and explained the situation to her and invited her to go with him. This woman of faith, overcoming her fear and anxiety at the prospect of leaving her family and the tranquillity of Becchi, said to her son: "If you think such a move is God's will, I'm ready to go right now."[6] Such an answer would come only from a woman of great faith in God and deep trust in her son!

On November 3, 1846, Mamma Margaret bade farewell to her sons Anthony and Joseph and to her grandchildren, and set out for Turin. She keenly felt the pain of leaving all behind to follow John, for whom she had labored so much to help him become a priest, and now she was to become a vital part of his ministry. Toward evening they arrived and entered their poor quarters—a few empty rooms. Here she would spend the last ten years of her life (1846–1856), making Valdocco a home for hundreds of abandoned youths. Some of the young boys, knowing of Don Bosco's arrival, came to welcome him; they also came to take a peek at this country woman whom they would soon call Mamma Margaret.

Don Bosco lost no time in carrying out his project. On Sundays he continued to welcome his boys, who now numbered about five-hundred. A number of diocesan priests were generous with their time and came to help him with the organizing, planning, and teaching. The laity also offered their services to benefit the poor and the abandoned. Afternoon classes were organized for catechism. Benefactors and admirers made contributions for prizes and awards. Eventually the premises became too small. Through the generosity of friends, John was able to purchase more land and expand the living quarters. Slowly he began to take in boarders who went off to school or work in the city. Mamma Margaret, with the help of other generous women, would look after the meals, the cleanliness, the mending, and the washing. John also assisted her whenever he had no other obligations.

Eventually, Don Bosco saw the need to provide education on site and began to build. Evening classes had already been organized and were popular—another example of how Don Bosco fulfilled his goal of building "good Christians and useful citizens." Public officials took notice and congratulated him for tackling the serious problem of illiteracy.

A number of boarders still went out to work at various jobs in the city. In 1855, Don Bosco introduced workshops on his own premises. The basic trades were taught. He became a pioneer in vocational training. He succeeded in this field long before the public schools of his day. His followers built up a network of such schools throughout the world, especially in Third World countries.

A Founder: Salesians of Don Bosco (SDB)

As his work expanded, Don Bosco needed helpers trained in his own philosophy, a blend of authentic humanism and Christian tradition. He was aware that his method of education was unconventional in his day. His entire approach was unique. Therefore, he began searching for suitable candidates among his

The Early Apostolate

own students and admirers, persons who showed signs of leadership and a willingness to be of service to the young. He began by assigning small responsibilities and by following their progress with suitable instruction and guidance. His plan and foresight bore fruit, but not without pain.

On January 26, 1854, Don Bosco invited four mature and dedicated young men to meet with him. He had been observing them closely for a few years, and he knew them well. He invited them to join him in his apostolic work for the young in the Oratory. Later, they would bind themselves with a promise and, if they so desired, take vows and join him more permanently. By his own wish, these followers of Don Bosco, were called Salesians because he greatly admired St. Francis de Sales (1567–1622), a Doctor of the Church and a Christian humanist who had practiced loving kindness in his own apostolate. Like Francis, Don Bosco based his apostolic thrust on love. He made the gentle bishop of Geneva a model for himself, for all who worked with him, and for all who would follow him. We already mentioned that Don Bosco named his first center *The Oratory of St. Francis de Sales.*

Don Bosco realized the need to establish a religious congregation which would perpetuate his mission. He was encouraged by the Holy Father, Pius IX, whom he had met already in 1858 and who was aware of his work in Turin. On December 18, 1859, the Salesian Congregation was officially established. Overcoming many obstacles and reverses, Don Bosco kept up his courage and his confidence in God along with great trust in Mary, the Help of Christians. On April 3, 1874, final approval was given by Rome. His mission was secure and firm.

All the while, the movement continued to grow. Centers were opened outside of Turin; the Salesian apostolate advanced into France, Spain, and England during the lifetime of Don Bosco. In 1875, he fulfilled another of his dreams by organizing his Congregation's first missionary expedition, which went to Argentina and eventually reached Patagonia at the tip of South America. Today the Salesian Missions are found all over the world. Don Bosco's philosophy of education was introduced into all cultures and has produced wonderful fruits; as Don Bosco said, he aimed to "make good Christians and useful citizens." Graduates of Salesian schools continue to attain leadership roles in all areas of society. His method of education easily adapts itself to all cultures because it carries the message of the Gospel. In January 1996, there were 17,500 Salesians in 1,770 centers scattered throughout the world.

Daughters of Mary Help of Christians
The Salesian Sisters (FMA)

"Why not do for girls what you are doing so well for the boys?" was the question that Don Bosco was hearing from all sides. Bishops and friends, aware of the success of his educational program, had been exerting pressure on him because of the great need for the care of girls. He was encouraged to found a congregation of women who would follow his educational philosophy and adapt it to girls. Don Bosco was slow to move, not wanting to be distracted from the work he was now doing. He kept telling himself: "I promised God that I would give myself to my last breath for poor boys."[7] In all his undertakings, Don Bosco sought only the will of God. Before embarking on this new venture, he sought heavenly inspiration, and it was not slow in coming.

On the night of July 5–6, 1862, Don Bosco had a dream that he was speaking to the Marchioness Barolo, a devout woman who used her wealth for the welfare of young girls living in the city of Turin. She urged him to give up his work for boys and devote himself exclusively to her institutions for girls. He told her emphatically that she could easily find chaplains for her institutions. He would not give up his boys, to whom he had dedicated his life after receiving a special call from on high.

Another dream came to him with a heavenly message. He found himself in one of Turin's large squares, and many girls were playing there. They ran up to the gentle priest and begged him to take care of them. Don Bosco tried to get away, telling them that he could not look after them and that others would care for them. But then the Lady of the first dream (1824) confronted him anew: "Take care of them; they are my children."[8]

A further sign would reach him in Fr. Dominic Pestarino (1817–1874), who came from Mornese, a small town seventy miles south of Turin. This good priest had organized a group of apostolic women who gathered the young girls of the town for recreation, sewing, and religious instruction. The girls were attracted by the welcoming and smiling young lady, Mary Mazzarello who was one of the outstanding members of a group called the Daughters of Mary Immaculate. Don Bosco met this group in the fall of 1864, on one of his autumn outings with his boys from Turin. He was impressed by the prayer life and apostolic zeal that energized this group. The moving spirit was Mary Mazzarello, who eventually became the group's leader. In her, Don Bosco saw a reflection of his own interior life and pastoral charity. He continued to mull over the many suggestions he had received to found an order of sisters who would follow his spirit. He thought that after all, he and Mary Mazzarello were kindred spirits.

From the favorable reports that he continued to receive from Mornese, Don Bosco eventually decided to move in the direction of founding a new congregation. He presented the project to the Council of the Salesians and gave them one month to reflect, pray, and come to a conclusion. The decision was unanimous in favor of the new project. He then went to Rome to seek the approval of Pius IX who encouraged him to move forward.

Earlier, the Pope had reminded him that women should not be neglected since they are a powerful factor in the work of redemption. He also remarked that it would be wrong to neglect the other half of humanity. The Foundation Day chosen was August 5, 1872, the Feast of Our Lady of the Snows. Mary figures prominently in so many milestones of the Salesian apostolate. On that day Mary Mazzarello and 15 young women received a religious habit from Don Bosco. Thus was born the Congregation of the Daughters of Mary Help of Christians, also known as the Salesian Sisters. In 1996 there were 16,452 Sisters in 1,533 centers scattered throughout the world, implementing the Salesian method of education and assisting young women to become good Christian mothers and nurturing, productive citizens.

Don Bosco—Writer and Publisher

Mindful of the special call he had received to assist youth and the working classes, Don Bosco took up the pen to promote spiritual, cultural, and human values. His own printing presses were used not only to teach the art of printing but also to publish more than one hundred works that came from his hand. His writings covered a variety of subjects: history, arithmetic, biographies, religion, monthly Catholic readings, plus a yearly almanac. A historical trilogy was his chief contribution to the literature of the time: *Church History* (1845), *Bible History* (1847), *History of Italy* (1855–1856). By general consensus Don Bosco's *History of Italy* is acknowledged as the masterpiece of all his works. Many sections of this volume were translated into English and used in the curriculum of European history in British schools.

Don Bosco's concern for the working classes led him to publish a simple explanation of the metric system of weights and measures. France had adopted this system at the turn of the century: other European nations, after some delay, followed suit. A year before the use of this system became law in Italy (1850), Don Bosco published a pamphlet, *"The Metric System Made Easy for the Farmer and the Workingman."* There was great demand for this pamphlet and several editions were printed. He then went a step further and prepared a three-act comedy that amusingly illustrated the new system to a packed house of distinguished visitors on December 15, 1849.

As a student, John loved books and was a voracious reader. He became friends with a Jewish bookseller called Elizah. For a very small fee John could borrow books and return them as soon as he had read them. John read a volume a day from what was called "The Popular Library Series." Toward the end of his high school years, he began to read the Latin classics. This love for books never left him. When the Oratory school was established, Don Bosco published a suitable collection of *Italian Classics for Young Readers.* This was soon followed by a series of the Latin classics. In 1870, Don Bosco presented Pope Pius IX with an elegantly bound copy of the Italian anthology. The Pope expressed great pleasure on receiving this gift. The Salesians today have as one of their apostolates the writing, publishing, and distribution of good books—continuing the tradition left to them by their Founder.

In his monthly Catholic Readings, Don Bosco wrote a series under the title, "Lives of the Popes in the First Centuries." These were concise biographies of the first twenty-one Popes. The author had a great love for the Church in the person of the Holy Father. In his own lifetime the Papacy was under attack from various quarters. Pius IX was at center stage in the political upheaval that removed the Papal States from the map and ultimately achieved the unification of Italy with Rome as its capital.

During this turbulent period Don Bosco stayed close to the Holy Father, who called on him for delicate diplomatic missions. Statesmen held Don Bosco in high esteem. He was entrusted with the delicate task of negotiating with the new government in the appointment of bishops to many vacant dioceses. The Pope would not act without seeking Don Bosco's advice on vexing problems. In all this, Don Bosco acted for the good of the Church and the betterment of society.

Looking Forward

In Chapter 1, we presented an overview of the problems facing society and today's youth: drugs, crime, sexual freedom, breakdown of the family, racial and social discrimination. Our society is witnessing the effects of unbelief and a consequent decline in moral and ethical values. A wave of pessimism and negativity pervades our society and affects the lives of the young.

In Chapters 2 and 3, we went back to the middle of the nineteenth century and saw how the Italian city of Turin was caught in a political crisis, with the government more concerned about raising money for armaments than caring for youth or improving society. This situation was exacerbated by the stress of the Industrial Revolution, which in Italy was centered in Turin. The rampant poverty of the rural and mountain regions forced many young people to seek the imaginary security and wealth of the city. With this migration there came countless moral and social problems.

But there was born into that era a man who, by temperament and grace, was destined to become one of its greatest educators. Appalled by what he saw around him Don Bosco decided to do something to stem the tide and prepare for a better future. He developed an educational approach that met the needs of the time. He called his method the *preventive system,* a term he adopted from the educational terminology of his day.

It is now time for us to pause and give an overview of educational theory and practice during the nineteenth century and ask ourselves what is Don Bosco's place in the history of education. To put his contribution in perspective, we must consider what had been going on at the end of the eighteenth century. Then we will describe the views of some nineteenth-century philosophers and educators, both secular and Christian. We hope this will help give Don Bosco his rightful place in education and make clear his contribution.

CHAPTER 3

1. Bosco, *Memoirs,* 182.
2. Ibid.
3. Auffray, *Saint John Bosco,* 55–57.
4. *Constitutions and Regulations of the Society of St. Francis de Sales* (Rome, Italy: Direzione Generale, Opere Don Bosco, 1984), c. 40, 43.
5. Bosco, *Memoirs,* 255.
6. Ibid., 296.
7. Ceria, *Don Bosco,* 258.
8. Morand Wirth, SDB, *Don Bosco and the Salesians* (New Rochelle, NY: Don Bosco Publications, 1982), 164.

4 Don Bosco in the History of Education

Before the dawn of the nineteenth century the man who had the greatest influence on education was Jean-Jacques Rousseau (1712–1778), the French philosopher and writer. His basic tenets regarding man and education are found in his novel *Emile*. For Rousseau, man was a reasonable being, emotional and affectionate, a child of nature, subject only to man's law, tolerant of all ideas, lord of an attractive universe. For him there was no original sin; the notion of grace and the supernatural had no meaning. He had great influence not only on the Enlightenment but also on the cult of rationalism—mankind can rely safely on natural feelings as a guide to conduct. Naturalism became the hallmark of the *new education*. He had many followers.

Among the disciples of Rousseau there was the renowned Swiss educator Johann Heinrich Pestalozzi (1746–1827). A charismatic educator, he stressed the climate of love more than the teaching of subjects. His dominant theme was *reaching the heart of the child*. Pestalozzi tried to create a family atmosphere. He emphasized maintaining good order without harshness. He encouraged good habits and considered education the means for the betterment of humanity. His book *How Gertrude Teaches Her Children* (1801) was a literary success, and his fame as an educator rested principally on that book. As with Rousseau, it must also be noted that his philosophy lacks the moral and religious dimension. Pestalozzi and his mentor, Rousseau, spoke always of *the child*. For Don Bosco, however, the all-important element of true education was to bring *Christ* into the heart of the child; this was the *raison d'être* of his pastoral mission and educational philosophy. Like Pestalozzi, Don Bosco kept emphasizing the importance of winning the hearts of students. "Education is a matter of the heart," he repeated.

Pestalozzi also influenced the German philosopher and educator Johann Friedrich Herbart (1776–1841) who made a notable contribution in the field of teaching methods. His efforts greatly helped to develop education into a science. He organized the procedures for lesson planning and left to history what is known as the "Herbartian steps": preparation, comparison or association, generalization, application.

On this side of the Atlantic, America can boast of the nineteenth-century educator Horace Mann (1796–1859) who championed universal education as an essential to democracy. His efforts on behalf of public schools made him one of the chief architects of modern education in the United States.[1] He visited most countries of Europe to study pedagogical practices and brought back the best to this country. He was an admirer of Johann Pestalozzi and, like him, advocated the humane treatment of the child. At the same time, he questioned the validity of punishment, which was so prevalent in European schools. It is interesting to note that Don Bosco also opposed the practice of physical punishment as characteristic of the *repressive system*. Don Bosco wholeheartedly endorsed the more humane and reasonable method that was called the *preventive system*, to which he added so much that in time he became identified with it. This approach to the education of youth is the one practiced by followers of Don Bosco.

In England Herbert Spencer (1820–1903) wrote an essay "What Education Is of Most Worth?" This piece, which came out in 1859, was published in the *Westminster Review* and stirred much debate in educational circles. Spencer's concern was to prepare the child for complete living. He questioned the classical curriculum; he promoted the vocational training movement. We will see later that Don Bosco also was a pioneer of vocational training.

In Italy, at the Royal University of Turin, the leading professor of education was Ferrante Aporti (1791–1858) who was influenced by Johann Pestalozzi. Aporti had high regard for Don Bosco and his down-to-earth approach to education, especially his insistence on reaching the heart of the young through the use of reasonable dialogue, loving kindness, and moral education and persuasion.

Don Bosco followed the lectures given by Aporti in Turin during the summer and fall of 1848. It is possible that Don Bosco came in contact with the theories of Pestalozzi through Aporti. There are some similarities between Aporti and Don Bosco: respect for the child, the method of benevolence and loving kindness, the reliance on persuasion; in short, the *preventive* idea. (Braido, 1989, p. 65.) Aporti was a staunch supporter of Don Bosco's educational method, which he witnessed on occasional visits to his schools. (Ribotta.)

Other professors at the University of Turin also admired Don Bosco's work. We may mention G. A. Raineri and G. Allievo, who had dealings with Don Bosco and his Oratories and endorsed his methods. Raineri advised his students to go to Valdocco, the poorest section of Turin, where Don Bosco's school was located. There they would observe practical techniques of instruction, all based on a sound philosophy of education coupled with Christian principles.[2]

Don Bosco drew from many sources and chose the best; nevertheless, we should not lose sight of his originality. One writer put it this way: "While Don Bosco had drawn from diverse historical, philosophical, and contemporary pedagogical sources to formulate his method, he rarely elaborated beyond brief outlines and notes for the passing of his system. Particularly as his work became more complex, he still allowed for flexibility in adapting his method according to circumstances or to allow for other successful methodology."[3]

Christian Educational Influences in the Nineteenth Century

Though significant in the history of education, Don Bosco was not an isolated figure. The *preventive system* that he adopted was also being followed by other outstanding educators. These dedicated men and women had similar intuitions and experiences in the practice of pedagogy, and they were not geographically far removed from the Turin priest. In both Italy and France there arose other proponents of a Christian educational approach based on the Gospel of love. Don Bosco could have been influenced by their writings, and could have been acquainted with their institutions.[4] In Venice, during the first decade of the nineteenth century, the Cavanis brothers (Antonio Angelo and Marco Antonio) dedicated themselves to the teaching of poor youth; and their apostolic work was carried on by a religious congregation that they founded, the Clerics of the Schools of Charity. Its members were encouraged to be more like fathers than teachers, and they were called upon to use the utmost charity in their work of education. Their goal was to teach Christian living by attracting the young to their Oratories, which were places of prayer, study, religious instruction, and recreation. We find similar objectives and goals in the writings and daily practice of Don Bosco.

In Brescia, a city located between Milan and Venice, we find a nobleman who became a priest, Fr. Lodovico Pavoni (1784–1849). He became one of the outstanding protagonists of the preventive approach in the education of youth. He too founded a religious congregation to perpetuate his initiatives, the Sons of Mary Immaculate. Like Don Bosco, Fr. Pavoni made it clear that his schools for the poor and abandoned were to become "places of Christian living . . . to teach them to become useful to the Church and to society . . . giving to the Church excellent Christians and skilled workers to society, virtuous and faithful members."[5] On the subject of discipline, Fr. Pavoni reminds his followers to use discretion in punishing minor infractions that stem from youthful mischief, irresponsibility, and thoughtlessness. The writings of Don Bosco run in the same vein.

In France, the Marist Brothers were founded in the year 1817 by Fr. Marcellin Champagnat (1789–1840), an outstanding protagonist of traditional Christian education in which an ounce of prevention is considered worth a pound of cure. He valued religious instruction as a way to inculcate right living and achieve the formation of the heart, conscience, and will. Fr. Champagnat had a special love for the Virgin Mary and presented her as a model to his sons: "The brothers will take as a model the Virgin Mary who teaches and serves the Child Jesus. Above all, they have to follow the way of love even in discipline, whose object is not to break the bruised reed by the power and fear of punishment, but to preserve always from evil, to correct faults, and to form the will."[6] The family spirit was to reign amid respect, love, confidence, but not fear!

There existed also dedicated women who gave their time and talents to the education of young women of all classes and in particular the disadvantaged. Outstanding in France were the members of the Society of the Sacred Heart, founded by Sophia Barat. Her basic principle was the practice of charity, and her followers took the *preventive* approach in contrast to the *repressive*. "The great pedagogues never ignored the fact that severity is neither the primary nor the perfect educational method; so that we often receive the impression that severity is only a means imposed by pedagogical incompetency. The excessive stressing of authority arises from weakness.... Pronouncements against severity in education are to be found in the works of the most varied authors, in St. Marie-Madeleine Barat no less than in Don Bosco."[7]

Another contribution was made by a zealous and generous lady, Teresa Eustochio Verzeri (1801–1852), from the city of

Bergamo, in northern Italy. This generous woman gave her all for the education of poor girls. To continue her work, in 1831 she founded a religious congregation called the Daughters of the Sacred Heart of Jesus. She left her daughters many nuggets of Christian pedagogical philosophy: '"Use extreme discretion and reasonableness . . ." 'Do not demand too much of your girls . . .' 'In general use loving-kindness, graciousness, vigilance, discretion, zeal.' 'Do not make them consider self-denial as sad and bitter as it appears, but as something reasonable, seasoned with sweetness and grace, and as something lightened by the Lord's hand.' 'Be kind and gentle and with loving-kindness and suffering you will obtain a thousand times more than you would with severity and fear.'"[8]

Fr. Leonardo Murialdo (1828–1900) was a dear friend and helper of Don Bosco in Turin. From 1857 to 1865, he took charge of the Oratory of Saint Aloysius, near Porta Nuova, the main railroad station. Early in life he was saddened to observe a growing rift between the European political leadership and the Church. In taking over the famous trade-apprentice school in Turin (*Collegio degli Artigianelli*) he redefined the scope of this Christian institution: '"To promote the moral and civil good of the working class, making honest and virtuous citizens out of many poor boys who, left to themselves, would all too easily become the shame and the scourge of society.' 'Our system during these thirty years has made hundreds of boys honorable in this world and has put them on the road to Paradise.'"[9]

The figure of Blessed Louis Guanella (1842–1915) is dear to Salesians. Already ordained a priest, he came to live with Don Bosco and stayed four years (1875–1878) at the Oratory, where he absorbed many Salesian ideas and made them his own. Discerning a call to a special mission, he left Don Bosco, but they remained always on friendly terms. He founded the Congregation of the Daughters of St. Mary of Providence for women and then the Servants of Charity for men. Their mission of apostolic love moved them to work for the poor and handicapped. He was inspired by St. Joseph Cottolengo, who had worked for the sick and incurable. Blessed Louis Guanella kept repeating "It is better to sin by indulgence than by rigor." "Let them always try to be loved, never or almost never to be feared."[10]

Don Bosco repeated often that "Education is a matter of the heart." To win the hearts of countless youngsters, he used a three-pronged approach: reason, religion, and kindness. We find in France a great educator who had the same idea. Fr. Pierre-Antoine Poullet (1810–1846), speaking of boarding school, says: "If the institution is not a family, it is nothing . . . love must occupy the first place in education. It is above all with the heart, with a loving, tender, and generous heart, that a teacher must fulfill his important mission." "Poullet is very clear about the purpose of education: to form the human and Christian character of the young. For him and other Christian educators, as we have been showing, the religious dimension is the main objective of education. Fulfillment of duties to God must be coupled with seriousness in study, which is itself a prayer, and therefore a religious and holy obligation."[11]

The same doctrine of *preventive* education was espoused by Felix Dupanloux (1849–1878), Bishop of Orleans, France. He insists that Christian education should forestall evil and inculcate the practice of virtue through example and instruction. Religious education for him was the primary objective, as it was in the centers run by Fr. Joseph Timon-David (1823–1893) in Marseilles. We find in Timon-David's methodology a happy balance of prayer life and religious instruction, education, recreation, and cultural activities such as music and singing.

To conclude this overview of the nineteenth-century educational movements that influenced Don Bosco, I would like to quote a review by Fr. Arthur Lenti, SDB, lecturer and professor at the Institute of Salesian Studies (Berkeley, California). Commenting on a recent study by Giochino Barzaghi, "Understanding Don Bosco in the Context of the Religious Culture of the Catholic Restoration" (1988), Fr. Lenti writes: "In any case, Barzaghi's interesting and intriguing study alerts us to the fact that Don Bosco was neither the first nor the only educator to face the problem of the education of the young, especially those needy and poor, and to advert to the necessity of a new way of approaching the problem. It also admonishes the student that Don Bosco's achievement in education, unique and great though it is, cannot be understood in isolation, but is best explained in the wider context of similar, if not quite as successful, experiments."[12]

Having reviewed the influences that secular and especially Christian educators had on St. John Bosco, we will now develop the three basic tenets of his pastoral and educational mission: *reason, religion, kindness*. Chapters 5, 6, and 7 will analyze the *preventive method*.

CHAPTER 4

1. *Colliers Encyclopedia*, vol. 15 (New York: Macmillan, 1985), 351.
2. Avallone, *Reason, Religion, Kindness*, 28.
3. Mullaly, "Viability of the Preventive System," 21.
4. Pietro Braido, *Breve Storia del Sistema Preventivo* (Rome, Italy: Libreria Ateneo Salesiano, 1993), 76.
5. Ibid., 78.
6. Ibid., 81.
7. Rudolf Allers, M.D., *The Psychology of Character* (London, England: Sheed and Ward, 1939), 62.
8. Braido, *Breve Storia*, 36.
9. Ibid., 42.
10. Ibid., 44.
11. Ibid., 71.
12. Arthur J. Lenti, SDB, "Essay Review," *Journal of Salesian Studies* 5, no. 2 (fall 1994): 122.

5 Reason: Being Reasonable with the Young

St. John Bosco's system of education has been aptly described as a *system of expression* and not *repression*. These words echoed in New York's St. Patrick's Cathedral on February 16, 1930. The occasion was a celebration of Don Bosco's beatification, which had occurred the year before. The speaker was Rt. Rev. William Turner, Bishop of Buffalo: "Expression is better than repression and it is in these terms that I present the educational system of Don Bosco as more up to date than other systems that call themselves modern."[1] What a deep insight! Don Bosco called his method the *preventive system;* he could have called it the *method of expression!* What is the history, though, of this title that he actually used?

In the spring of 1877 Don Bosco went to Nice, France, to dedicate a new foundation called St. Peter's Hospice. There were many present, and among them some dignitaries. In his address, Don Bosco described the Salesian way of working with youth as helping them to become "good Christians and useful citizens." The audience was impressed. The welcome and warmth that his words received prompted him to have the speech printed under the title, *The Preventive System in the Education of the Young.* This booklet, produced by the printing shop at the Oratory, became a seminal document that inspired his many followers and admirers throughout the world.

Why, you ask, did Don Bosco adopt the word *preventive?* Other educators had already employed this term as part of an antithesis that Don Bosco noted in his speech at Nice: "There are two systems which have been in use through all ages in the education of youth: the preventive and the repressive."[2] The latter was more threatening and inclined to punishment: the words and looks of those in charge were always severe. In contrast, the style preferred by Don Bosco was marked by familiarity and kindness, gentle presence, open dialogue, and willing cooperation. Naturally, he espoused what was called the *preventive method.* The term, however, does not do justice to the richly creative and constructive approach he followed in teaching the young.

For Don Bosco, the choice of the adjective *preventive* was deliberate because it clearly described the path he had traveled already for thirty-six years. He could have chosen another term, but he did not do so. The term *preventive,* as used by Don Bosco, derives its meaning from the Latin verb *praevenire;* that is, to "foresee" and "provide." As a way of teaching, the *preventive system* calls for loving presence and constant availability. The aim is to encourage, counsel, and assist in personal growth and maturity.

In the next three chapters, I will describe this method of education that Don Bosco practiced and left in heritage to his sons and daughters. It is employed today in over one hundred countries to produce "good Christians and useful citizens."

The Meaning of Reason

One of the rewards with which Don Bosco encouraged his more deserving students was to take them on an outing in the rolling hills of Piedmont. These outings came to be known as the "autumn trips." As his apostolate began to be more widely known, he was blessed with a number of vocations to his congregation.

In the month of October 1864, Don Bosco and his boys were invited by the priest of the village of Mornese, about seventy miles south of Turin. This was also an opportunity for Don Bosco to become acquainted with a group of apostolic young women under the leadership of Mary Mazzarello, later to become the cofoundress of the Salesian Sisters, who would adapt Don Bosco's *preventive system* for the education of girls.

The local schoolmaster, Francis Bodrato, was impressed that the visiting youngsters showed respect and self-discipline while nonetheless enjoying a cheerful familiarity with their priest. Noticing the powerful sway of charity and realizing that he had much to learn from this man's method of education, he resolved to learn Don Bosco's secret in bending to his will a crowd of boys naturally intolerant of discipline. Francis asked Don Bosco for an interview, and Don Bosco obliged:

> Reason and Religion are the two springs of my method of education. An educator should realize that all these fine lads, or nearly all, are smart enough to sense the good done to them and are innately open to sentiments of gratitude. With God's help, we must strive to make them grasp the main tenets of our faith which, based entirely on love, reminds us of God's infinite love for mankind. We must seek to strike in their hearts a chord of gratitude which we owe Him in return for the benefits He so generously showers upon us. We must do our best to convince them through simple reasoning that gratitude to God means carrying out His will and obeying His commandments, especially those which stress observance of the duties of our state of life. Believe me, if our efforts succeed, we have accomplished the greater part of our educational task. . . . The secret of my method of education is summed up in two words: religion and reason—religion, genuine and sincere, to control one's actions; reason, to apply moral principles to one's activities rightly.[3]

The question remains: What is really meant by *expression and not repression?* As stated previously, three principles are the foundation of this educational method. The first and most natural principle is the use of "reason" or "reasonableness"—a basic postulate in any educational undertaking. Don Bosco insisted that reason must dominate and inspire all one's actions: "Reason and religion are the means an educator must constantly apply; he must teach them and himself practice them if he wishes to be obeyed and to attain his end."[4] I might add that reason should be practiced by every parent from the beginning of a child's life.

In stating that reason is a fundamental principle of his system, Don Bosco is not saying anything original. No genuine education can be imparted without the constant use of reason. This nineteenth century educator wanted to focus on the need for good common sense in education; he was challenging the accepted style of pedagogy, in which the teacher was a hard taskmaster who was quick to use the rod, with little time for rhyme or reason in working with youth. This approach was unacceptable to Don Bosco. He wanted the young to express themselves, to reason out the purpose and need for judicious discipline when the time called for it. The cultivation of an open and spontaneous attitude, he felt, is of prime importance in the maturation of the young.

This mindset is healthy and psychologically sound. True education always seeks to foster and develop such an attitude and mentality. To reach this goal, one who wants to influence the young and assist in their development must understand what it means to be reasonable. Reasonableness begins with oneself and then leads to consistency in applying reason in dealing with others, especially the young who so often act thoughtlessly and impulsively.

Gifted by nature and graced by the Spirit, John followed his natural inclinations and intuitive educational awakenings in the pursuit of his goal, inspired by heaven in the boyhood vision/dream of 1824. In writing his pamphlet, Don Bosco aimed to crystallize in summary form the guidelines that he had followed and practiced in his own ministry, which had attracted many followers. Won over to his plan, these men and women dedicated their time and energy to the betterment of society in developing "good Christians and useful citizens."

The Teacher—a Bridge

A keen insight regarding a leader of the young—whether he/she leads as a teacher or in some other capacity—comes to us from an Australian writer. In his recent study on the Salesian way of education, "Walking with the Young," Rev. Patrick Laws, SDB, remarks: "Anyone called to youth must become a bridge over which students pass in the voyage of discovery of the world. . . . The alternative for them is to brave uncharted waters."[5]

To become a bridge demands constant presence and open dialogue with youth, to listen to every question before attempting an answer. This implies a deep respect for the young and a willingness to spend time with them in order to get to know them. To indicate by a welcoming smile that one is approachable and to be available for dialogue calls for love on the part of one called to be an educator: "An educator is one who is entirely consecrated to the welfare of his pupils, and should, therefore, be ready to face every difficulty and endure fatigue in order to obtain his object, which is the civil, moral and intellectual education of his pupils. . . . Remember, however, all need patience, diligence, and prayer, without which I believe all rule is unavailing."[6]

The three words above (*patience, diligence, prayer*) are indicative of the high esteem in which Don Bosco held educators. In another section of this document he states: "Hence only a Christian can apply the 'Preventive' system with success." He makes that statement after giving the basis on which his method rests: "The practice of this system is wholly based on the words of St. Paul who says: 'Caritas patiens est, benigna est. Omnia suffert, omnia sperat, omnia sustinet' (I Cor. xiii, 4, 7)—'Charity is patient, is kind. It beareth all things, hopeth all things, endureth all things.'"[7]

Don Bosco used these three key words to emphasize the basic qualities of a good teacher. "Patience" echoes the words of St. Paul when he says "Charity is patient . . . it bears all things." Then Don Bosco speaks of "diligence," which takes its origin from the Latin word *diligere* (to love). An educator learns to love one's work and puts all one's energy and generosity and dedication into it. Finally, Don Bosco stresses the need for prayer, which calls for faith in the power of the Spirit to change hearts. "All educators should strive to imitate this divine example of Jesus and model their zeal after His. Then they will give corrections at the proper time, in all enlightenment and charity, after waiting patiently in the name of God for the moment of grace."[8]

The Second Vatican Council (1962–1965) speaks eloquently of the vocation of a teacher who is qualified and skilled in the art of education and knows how to use all modern techniques. The Council fathers speak also of teachers "possessed by charity both towards each other and towards their pupils, and inspired by an apostolic spirit, they should bear testimony by their lives and their teaching to the one Teacher, who is Christ. Splendid, therefore, and of the highest importance is the vocation of those who help parents in carrying out their duties and act in the name of the community by undertaking a teaching career. This vocation requires special qualities of mind and heart. . . ."[9]

A Forerunner of Youth Activities

Today we are witnessing the sad plight of the young who have too much time on their hands: they get into all kinds of trouble. Again and again, we see how true it is that "an empty mind becomes the devil's workshop." It was by no means accidental that Don Bosco emphasized providing healthy activities for youth as one of the foundations of his method. Let me quote the words of a great American, Alfred Smith (former governor of New York State and presidential candidate in 1928). He said of Don Bosco, "He clearly saw the needs of youth and proposed and practiced a system of education well suited to their age and nature. . . . This system aims at the free and spontaneous development of a child's energies."[10]

In the Crime Bill recently passed by the U.S. Congress (September 1994) and signed by President Clinton, there is a clause providing funding for "midnight basketball." This provision aims at keeping the young off the streets at night and deterring them from crime by keeping them busy in wholesome recreation. Local law enforcement officers would have much to say on this score.

Today's youth activities—sports, music, drama, debating, various forms of competition—are wholesome means of growth in personality and confidence. The need for new experiences is also met, with the added advantage of promoting discipline and human relationships. Likewise, the need for attention is fulfilled by these multiple activities. Better to expend the energies of the young in healthy ways than to allow them to destroy themselves through the use of drugs or violence.

The Home

In his book *Five Cries of Youth*, Merton Strommen identifies "self-hatred" as the first cry: "Feelings of worthlessness often make people turn on themselves in anger. Then the cry becomes a mixture of worthlessness, self-hatred, and loneliness. As the most commonly voiced and the most intensely felt of the five cries, it is the first to be discussed."[11] This phenomenon proceeds from feelings of worthlessness, self criticism, and loneliness. Feelings of worthlessness often make a person turn on himself or herself. Efforts by interested persons to reach out into meaningful dialogue often prove useless.

What is needed is a change in perception; this change can bring about a change in feelings. The family has a primary function in bringing about this change. It is not an impossible task. It seems most important that we begin with a clear statement of the needs of the adolescent: belonging, security, affirmation, attention, new experiences. And it is primarily in the home, in an affirming family, that these needs are met.

In Robert Frost's poem "The Death of the Hired Man," two characters each try to define the word *home*. The first defines it as a kind of necessity: within its walls there is no warmth, no kindness.

> Home is the place where, when you have to go there, They have to take you in.

But, the second character envisions home as a place of peace and joy.

> I should have called it Something you somehow haven't to deserve.[12]

The home environment does make a lot of difference. Today social scientists tell us that about fifty percent of American households are one-parent homes. This problem must be faced by social agencies and by all those involved in the care and training of youth. All must salvage what they can and get on with life. A striking observation was made at a gathering of San Francisco therapists discussing sexual abuse. Mardi Horowitz, a professor at the California University in San Francisco, said: "The point is to move into the future and have as satisfying a life as you can. Don't sit in the bus looking out the rear window. Get in the driver's seat!"[13]

Today we hear constantly the word *environment*. We are challenged to sustain our forests, keep our rivers and streams clean, and preserve our endangered species. In his first letter to youth, issued on Palm Sunday 1985, Pope John Paul mentioned that one of the deepest concerns of youth is for their elders to preserve the environment until they grow up to become stewards of it in turn.

The first element of Salesian education, as outlined by St. John Bosco, is reason. This abstract concept has several dimensions. First, it calls attention to the common sense aspect of interpersonal relationships. It implies the need for dialogue and communication with the young in order to understand and guide them. The basis of this process is a friendship that has to be cultivated. To be able to meet the needs of youth requires knowledge of their ways, their attitudes, and their inclinations. The following anecdote will help illustrate this.

On April 25, 1884, in Rome, Don Bosco was approached by a reporter from a French newspaper. After some questions about Don Bosco's ability to establish so many institutions and the secret of his resources, the following dialogue took place:

REPORTER: Don Bosco, would you please tell me in what your educational system consists?

DON BOSCO: Very simple! Let the young have full liberty to do the things that are pleasing to them. The secret is to discover their potential, their abilities. Then seek to develop them. Each one does with pleasure only what he knows he can accomplish. I follow this principle. My students work not only energetically but with love. In forty-six years I have not used any punishment, and I can assure you that many students love me.

REPORTER: Don Bosco, your system is truly wonderful![14]

The secret is *presence,* to spend time with youth, to be actively present among them. To enter their world of games and sports and music is the key to an understanding of their values and an ability to lead them to greater, higher, values; and eventually, spiritual ones. As Don Bosco would say: "We love the things they love and then bring them to love the things we love." The teacher or leader becomes the friend who is then respected, loved, and admired; he is an accepting person, quick to praise and slow to condemn. The Salesian educator guides gently but firmly as a true friend on the road to Christian maturity. John Paul II also highlighted the value of this educational presence when he addressed the Salesians in his letter *"Juvenum Patris"*:

The true educator therefore shares the life of the young, is interested in their problems, tries to become aware of how they see things, takes part in their sporting and cultural activities and in their conversations: as a mature and responsible friend he sketches out for them ways and means of doing good, he is ready to intervene to solve problems, to indicate criteria, to correct with prudent and loving firmness blameworthy judgments and behavior. In this atmosphere of "pedagogical presence" the educator is not looked upon as a "superior," but as a "father, brother and friend."[15]

The words of Don Bosco are clear:

By the Preventive System pupils acquire a better understanding, so that an educator can speak to them in the language of the heart, not only during the time of their education but even afterwards. Having once succeeded in gaining the confidence of his pupils he can subsequently exercise a great influence over them, and counsel them, advise and even correct them, whatever position they may occupy in the world later on.[16]

The philosophy underpinning the "reason" dimension of Don Bosco's method is crystallized in article thirty-eight of the Constitutions (guidelines) of the worldwide Salesian Congregation; the spirit described is adhered to by all the members of the Salesian Family as well as admirers of this nineteenth-century educator. I will quote this article in its entirety as a conclusion to this chapter.

Don Bosco has handed on to us his Preventive System as a means for carrying out our educational and pastoral service.
    This system is based entirely on reason, religion and loving kindness. Instead of constraint, it appeals to the resources of intelligence, love and the desire for God, which everyone has in the depths of his being.
    It brings together educators and youngsters in a family experience of trust and dialogue.
    Imitating God's patience, we encounter the young at their present stage of freedom. We then accompany them, so that they may develop solid convictions and gradually assume the respon-

sibility for the delicate process of their growth as human beings and as men of faith.[17]

CHAPTER 5

1. William Turner, "Expression not Repression!" panegyric of Blessed John Bosco's educational system, delivered in St. Patrick's Cathedral, New York City (Privately printed, New York, 1930), 10.
2. "The Preventive System in the Education of the Young" in *Constitutions and Regulations of the Society of St. Francis de Sales* (Rome, Italy: Direzione Generale Opere Don Bosco, 1984), 246.
3. Lemoyne, *Biographical Memoirs,* VII: 451.
4. *Constitutions and Regulations of the Society of St. Francis de Sales,* 249
5. Patrick Laws, *Walking with the Young* (Manila, Philippine Islands: Salesiana Publishers, 1993), 12.
6. *Constitutions and Regulations of the Society of St. Francis de Sales* (London, England: The Salesian Press, 1949), 40, 45.
7. Ibid., 36.
8. Avallone, *Reason, Religion, Kindness,* 88.
9. "Declaration on Christian Education," in *Vatican Council II, The Conciliar and Post Conciliar Documents,* ed. Austin Flannery (Northport, NY: Costello Publishing Co., 1975), no. 8, 732, no. 5, 730.
10. Neil Boyton, foreword to *The Blessed Friend of Youth* (New York: Macmillan Co., 1945).
11. Strommen, *Five Cries,* 7–8.
12. *The Oxford Book of American Verse,* ed. F. O. Matthiessen (Oxford, England: The Clarendon Press, 1950), 553.
13. *San Francisco Chronicle,* 17 October 1994, A 15–16.
14. Ceria, *Memorie Biografiche,* 17: 85–86.
15. Pope John Paul II, "*Juvenum Patris,*" 25.
16. *Constitutions and Regulations of the Society of St. Francis de Sales,* 1984, 248.
17. Ibid., c. 38, 42.

6 Religion: Walking with the Young to Christ

"And people were bringing children to Him that He might touch them, but the disciples rebuked them. When Jesus saw this He became indignant and said to them: 'Let the children come to me; do not prevent them, for the kingdom of God belongs to such as these. Amen, I say to you, whoever does not accept the kingdom of God like a child will not enter it.' Then He embraced them and blessed them, placing His hands on them."[1]

This same attitude toward youth is found in Pope John Paul II, "the sweet Christ on earth," to use an expression that St. Catherine of Siena employed when referring to another Pope. John Paul's unprecedented number of journeys are characterized, among other things, by the great emphasis he places on youth rallies. The unforgettable journey to Denver, Colorado, in August 1993 drew over two hundred thousand teenagers from five continents. It was unheard of that such a multitude of young people could be together without major disorder—much to the amazement of the Denver police and security officers. The secret of this phenomenon was the moral and religious background of these young people, who made us all stand tall and proud. The final words of John Paul to the large assembly were: "Be proud of your faith!"

St. John Bosco often said, with emphasis, "My method is based on *Reason* and *Religion*." In this chapter, our focus will shift to the second element of Don Bosco's educational approach: Religion. I decided to give this chapter a more comprehensive title: "Religion: Walking the Journey of Faith with the Young." The faith that came to us in Baptism needs to be exercised and must lead to a holy and spiritual life, as an essential part of an integral education. Don Bosco could not consider an education complete without a firm basis in religion—that is, believing and living one's faith through worship of God in the Church, to be followed by an effort to build Christian community in service to all our brothers and sisters. The journey of faith calls for this service, which is a necessary dimension for those striving for holiness of life.

Youth Called to Holiness

There is only one spirituality and that consists in following the Gospel as outlined in the Beatitudes. In September 1988, Pope John Paul II went to Becchi (twenty miles from Turin) to visit John Bosco's birthplace. He named the hillside that faces the grand Basilica the Hill of the Beatitudes of Youth to designate the holiness of the place where John began his journey to holiness through the grace of the Spirit. It was also here that John began his apostolic work with the young people of his neighborhood. The word *Salesian* refers to St. Francis de Sales, who wrote so much about the universal call to holiness. It was in the spirit and according to the teachings of this Saint that Don Bosco, faithful to his first prophetic dream, strove to develop holiness of life in the young people to whom he reached out.

We keep coming back to the historical-prophetic boyhood dream or vision of 1824. The words of the Good Shepherd remained impressed on John's mind and moved his heart to action; these words became in time the charter of his apostolic mission: "You will have to win these friends of yours not by blows but by gentleness and love. Start right away to teach them the ugliness of sin and the value of virtue."[2] The message of this dream became the inspiration of his life. For Don Bosco and his followers, education was a matter of the heart; the journey of life was to be traveled with a new heart, one transformed by moral and spiritual values. "True education is directed towards the formation of the human person in view of his final end and the good of that society to which he belongs and in the duties of which he will, as an adult, have a share."[3] This teaching of the Second Vatican Council echoes what we have said over and over: Don Bosco's educational philosophy aims to produce "good Christians and useful citizens."

The present chapter will emphasize the need for moral values and religious training in the *preventive system*. However, it must be pointed out that Don Bosco did not minimize in any way the importance of the physical, intellectual, emotional, and social dimensions of education. Good psychologist that he was, he aimed to educate the whole person, to make him/her a good and useful citizen who would help create a better society. For him, the only way to achieve this goal was through religious and moral principles of action. The General Chapters of both Congregations (The Salesians and the Sisters) convene every six years and reaffirm this philosophy; members from all over the world strive to update the *preventive system* and keep it relevant and attractive to a rapidly changing world.

Pope John Paul called upon the followers of St. John Bosco to renew their vocation to foster youth holiness. In 1988 the Holy Father wrote a letter to the Salesians and to all the members of the Salesian Family on the centennial of the death of the Saint. Entitled "*Juvenum Patris*" (Father of Youth), this message was a reminder to the worldwide Salesian Family to return to the *preventive system,* with special emphasis on making youth aware of their call to holiness by cultivating the seeds of spiritual life already planted in Baptism. "For St. John Bosco, founder of a great spiritual family, one may say that the peculiar trait of his brilliance is linked with the educational method which he himself called the '*preventive system.*' [Italics mine] In a certain sense this represents the quintessence of his pedagogical wisdom and constitutes the prophetic message which he left to his followers and to the Church."[4]

> ... the integral educative mission that we see incarnated in John Bosco is a realistic pedagogy of holiness. We need to get back to the true concept of *'holiness'* as a component of the life of every believer. The originality and boldness of the plan for a 'youthful holiness' is intrinsic to the educational art of this great saint, who can rightly be called the *'Master of Youth Spirituality.'* His secret lay in the fact that he did not disappoint the deep aspirations of the young (the need for life, love, expansiveness, joy, freedom, and future prospects) but at the same time led them gradually and realistically to discover for themselves that only in the *'life of grace'*, i.e., in friendship with Christ, does one fully attain the most authentic ideals.[5] [Italics mine]

Don Bosco realized his own holiness through an educative commitment that he lived with a burning zeal and an apostolic heart. The relationship between education and holiness was fundamental to his personal ideals. By the grace of the Spirit he became a holy educator. He lived and grew in a holy environment. His mother was a saintly woman. Don Bosco drew his inspiration from a saintly model, St. Francis de Sales. He was guided by a holy spiritual director, St. Joseph Cafasso. He discerned the holiness of St. Mary Domenica Mazzarello, the cofoundress of the Daughters of Mary Help of Christians, the Salesian Sisters. Under the inspiration of grace and influenced by the spirituality of Salesian education, two teenagers became outstanding for holiness of life: St. Dominic Savio (1842–1857), an early student of the Oratory, and Blessed Laura Vicuña (1891–1904), a pupil of the Salesian Sisters who gave her life for her mother. (Cf. *"Juvenum Patris,"* no. 5.)

The life of Dominic Savio offers insight into Don Bosco's ideal of spiritual education, especially since Don Bosco himself wrote a biography of the young Saint. I would like to select two episodes in particular. The first meeting between Don Bosco and Dominic took place at Murialdo, where Don Bosco had taken his boys for the history-making autumn outings. This encounter illustrates the true goal of all Salesian centers: to prepare citizens for this world and for eternity.

It was early in the morning of the first Monday of October 1854, when Don Bosco saw a young boy approaching with his father and was at once struck by his serene expression and cheerful but modest demeanor. The following dialogue ensued:

> DON BOSCO: What's your name? Where do you live?
>
> DOMINIC SAVIO: I'm Dominic Savio. I live in Mondonio. Fr. Cugliero, my teacher, told you about me.

Don Bosco asked him some questions about his home life and what he had learned up until then. Mutual confidence was established. The priest saw that the child was truly filled with the Holy Spirit and Don Bosco marvelled at the working of grace in one so young. After they had talked for some time and Don Bosco was about to speak to his father, Dominic asked:

> DOMINIC SAVIO: Will I do, Father? Will you take me to Turin to study?
>
> DON BOSCO: Well, you seem to have good stuff in you.
>
> DOMINIC SAVIO: Good stuff. Good for what?
>
> DON BOSCO: Good for a lovely vestment to give the Lord.
>
> DOMINIC SAVIO: Then you are the tailor and I'm the cloth. Take me with you and make me into a beautiful vestment for Him![6]

Don Bosco was convinced that moral values have a great influence on the mind and conduct of the young. While caring for the total person, he always stressed the spiritual dimension without trying to sound too pietistic. His aim was to encourage the young to think and act out of moral persuasion. He anticipated in practice what Pope Pius XI was to describe in one of the first great papal letters on education: "Christian education takes in the whole aggregate of human life, physical and spiritual, intellectual and moral, individual, domestic and social, not with a view of reducing it in any way, but in order to elevate, regulate, and perfect it in accordance with the example and teaching of Christ. Hence the true Christian, product of Christian education, is the supernatural man who thinks, judges and acts constantly and consistently in accordance with right reason illuminated by the supernatural light of the example and teaching of Christ. . . ."[7]

Don Bosco's inspiration has not been lost; it has been carried on by his spiritual sons and daughters. The Constitutions of the Salesian Sisters capture his spirit when they use the expression "walking with them [the young] in the path of holiness."[8]

Likewise the sons of Don Bosco are reminded that the most precious gift they can give to youth is an authentic witness of holiness through a daily living of the beatitudes, as "we walk side by side with the young."[9]

What is the essence of this youth holiness that John Paul II spoke about in his letter to the Salesian Family? Can this holiness be made attractive to today's youth, so caught up in secular and materialistic values? After all, the *preventive system* was written and practiced over a hundred years ago! We are living in a new age!

The Salesian Sisters and the Salesian Fathers today are working effectively in over one hundred countries. The Salesian educational philosophy is "transcultural" because it is not restricted by time or geography or ethnicity. It is based on three universal principles. First, the *preventive system* reasons with the young and those not so young. Second, it surrounds all persons with loving kindness without suffocating them; finally, it focuses on religious values as a motivating force. Don Bosco crystallized these principles in three words: *Reason, Religion, Kindness.* He summarized in one sentence the gleanings of fifty years of experience: "Remember, however, that all need patience, diligence, and prayer, without which I believe all rule is unavailing."[10]

Salesian Youth Holiness

Educators and other leaders of youth should keep before their eyes the Good Shepherd who searches for the lost sheep while tending the whole flock. Followers of Don Bosco's philosophy take the first step in approaching the young and traveling with them along the same road. While listening to them and sharing their hopes and anxieties, they patiently explain to them the meaning of the Gospel and its demands, while also sharing with them the peace and joy that fill their hearts in discipleship with Christ. This whole process is what is meant by the "journey of faith." The followers of John Bosco inspire the young to desire true life and live it to the full. As Salesian Cardinal Antonio M. Javierre Ortas put it: "Don Bosco with his system of education, which is none other than the Gospel at the service of education, will make your march toward your goal easier." Pope John Paul in his first letter to youth (1985) said: "Open yourselves to Christ, be genuine Christians. Through your life, radiate in all places the Gospel of Christ." The Holy Father was encouraging all youth to seek and develop a deep spiritual life.

To promote and foster the growth of the young to fullness of life after the measure of Christ, the Perfect Man, the Salesians in their 1990 General Chapter set forth a five-step program to help youth attain a deep and personal holiness. The term used was *spirituality* that is, a life of the spirit.[11] These words *holiness* and *spirituality* refer to the soul; they embrace individual religious convictions and attitudes. Emphasis is placed on the spiritual aspects of thought, life, and behavior. All this rests on belief in a Supreme Being. This faith guides believers to a life of moral virtue and lasting values.

We will now summarize those five steps.

■ **The holiness of ordinary life.** Reading the biography of Don Bosco leads to the conviction that he was clearly a man with both feet on the ground when it came to the education of the young. With great insistence on doing one's duty well and accepting the reality of one's situation, Don Bosco was preparing his youngsters for their place in society as good workers and honest citizens, capable of providing for themselves and for their families. Faithfulness to one's obligations is the highway to holiness.

Fr. Peter Braido, SDB, critical scholar and researcher of the life and times and writings of St. John Bosco, remarks that there was nothing naive about his kindness and gentleness. Don Bosco prepared his students for life, while stressing responsibilities and service to those in need. Developing a spiritual life was to be both a guiding light and a continuous support in life's struggles. Don Bosco encouraged constant trust in divine help—the result of fidelity to prayer and the sacramental life and devotion to Mary, the Mother of God.

■ **The joy and optimism of holiness.** Another part of the spiral movement in the process of education to the faith is called "the spirituality of joy and optimism." It is significant that the first words of the Second Vatican Council's Pastoral Constitution on The Church in the Modern World are "Joy and Hope."

On June 24, 1855, the boys of the Oratory celebrated the name day of Don Bosco. It was the Feast of St. John the Baptist. Don Bosco invited all the boys to write to him and ask for a gift, and he would provide it. Dominic Savio wrote to Don Bosco and asked his help to become a saint. Don Bosco repeated the formula that one must always be joyful and peaceful, while at the same time to attend to one's duties.[12]

In 1847, Don Bosco published a prayer book for youth, the first of its kind in Italy. Millions of copies were printed in his lifetime. The first pages of this *Companion of Youth* acknowledged the love and joy of life desired by the young. "I want you to be happy. I should like to teach you how to lead a life that will make you happy and contented." Don Bosco wanted to help the young realize that Baptism inserted them into the mystery of Salvation, the source and foundation of lasting peace and joy.

As a young student, John organized a group of friends who became known as the Merry Company, *La società dell'allegria*. This group was composed of youngsters who, under the leadership of John, knew how to combine study and prayer, duty and joy, obedience and respect for law and order. Mutual support was the bond that united this club, whose members found security and happiness in outings, games, hikes, sports. Such elements have always been valued in Salesian education as necessary tools of growth, maturation, and human development.

■ **Holiness is friendship with Christ.** Growth in faith moves individual souls to a special friendship with the Lord. We mentioned that among the fruits of hope we find joy and optimism. The rock foundation of all this is the life of grace, the spiritual help given to all believers to live the commandments and follow the beatitudes. The Salesian style of holiness is based on joy and optimism. Some experts in the field of youth holiness and spirituality might smile at this simple and perhaps innovative approach, concerned that it might lead to a playing down of the Gospel demands and the sacrifices that life requires. Far from it! John Paul II, visiting the birthplace of John Bosco on the occasion of the centennial year of his death (1988), called it the Hill of the Beatitudes of Youth because from that place there went forth a message of joy and commitment for all young people who look to Don Bosco as a *Father and Teacher* (XXIII General Chapter of the Salesians).

The Gospel message was what motivated Don Bosco to continue his mission. His personal love for Christ compelled him to bring Christ to the young and the young to Christ: Friend, Teacher, Redeemer. These three words describe the spiritual experience that can lead youth to find the center of their existence in Christ, who gives meaning to their life. Those for whom Christ has become central are able to make the Gospel message more meaningful to their friends and companions. Don Bosco's constant concern, therefore, was to educate to the faith, walking " . . . side by side with the young so as to lead them to the risen Lord, and so to discover in him and his gospel the deepest meaning of their own existence, and thus grow into new men."[13]

■ **Holiness and communion with the church.** In 1858, Don Bosco visited Rome for the first time and had an audience with the Holy Father, Pope Pius IX, who would authorize him to found the Salesian Congregation. Pius IX remembered the kindness of the Oratory boys who had made sacrifices in order to send him a modest contribution when he was in exile in Gaeta. Moved by their generosity, the Holy Father gave Don Bosco some money for refreshments for the poor boys. Don Bosco's purpose in encouraging the youngsters to send a gift to the Holy Father was to impress upon them the need for love and respect for the Holy Father as Vicar of Christ on earth and head of the universal Church.

Don Bosco's tireless zeal assisted the Pope to reestablish several Italian dioceses that had been closed by an anticlerical government. Don Bosco received many diocesan seminarians into his institutions so that they could complete their theological studies and become priests. More than one thousand priests were assisted in this way.

The founding of the congregations was intended to be of service to the Church by defending and spreading the faith especially among poor and abandoned youth, both at home and abroad. In 1875, the first Salesian missionary expedition was organized by Don Bosco who, in a dream, had seen his sons and daughters laboring among the Indians of South America, as well as among the citizens and the many immigrants there. Two years later, the Salesian Sisters also sent missionaries. The combined efforts of the two congregations have produced wonderful results in the work of evangelization through the establishment of churches, schools, and missions. The success of the missionary efforts was due to the Salesian style of action as outlined in Don Bosco's pastoral and educational method.

In our description of a five-step youth spirituality, we identified the third step as friendship with the Lord. Love for Christ leads us necessarily to love for His spouse, the Church. To put it another way, we say with the theologians "Christology guides our Ecclesiology." Youth spirituality finds its source and support in the Church founded by Christ. It is in the Church that youth finds the strength to grow and persevere in the Christian life. That is why Don Bosco, in the first prayer book he wrote for the young, inserted in the morning offering this phrase: "My God, I thank you for having created me, called me into your Church, and preserved me during the past night."

Love for the Church was one of three devotions that Don Bosco recommended to his followers. This love embraced the whole Church: its doctrine, creed, morality, and sacramental life; in other words, to believe, to practice, to receive the sacraments. This love for the Church expresses itself in fidelity to the authority of the Holy Father, successor of St. Peter, to whom Christ entrusted the *keys of the kingdom* and upon whom Christ founded his Church. Salesian Youth Spirituality includes an explicit love and veneration of the Pope and adherence to his teaching. The Holy Father is a visible sign of unity for the whole Church. He is a providential presence through the service he provides in the name of Christ the Lord for the benefit of all humanity.[14]

This relationship with Christ includes the celebration of the Sacraments. Salesian tradition the world over continues to stress their necessity for the Christian growth of youth. Don Bosco's key to holiness is the spiritual influence of the Sacrament of Reconciliation and the Eucharist, the main pillars of his educational philosophy.

The Sacrament of Reconciliation (Confession) was celebrated often at the Oratory. It was prepared for with a welcoming environment, rich in genuine fellowship and sincere friendship.

The openness of the young and the kindness of the confessors fused to prepare the soul for the grace of God if needed, or the deepening of this grace. Regular use of this sacrament continues the process of conversion and renewal, leading always to a deeper spirituality that frees one from selfishness and prepares individuals to share with others their friendship with Christ.

According to the Friend of Youth, the devout reception of the Holy Eucharist is the second pillar of education. Received with genuine faith and proper disposition of heart and soul, the Eucharist becomes a significant source of strength to live the commandments. The Bread of Life enkindles the desire for spiritual growth in the young, who are then inspired by the Spirit to imitate Christ's total self-giving and carry the Gospel message to their brothers and sisters. Through the Eucharist, individuals open themselves to the needs of others and commit themselves to apostolic activities in peer ministry. The Eucharist frequently received makes youth a channel of grace for others.

■ **The holiness of responsible service.** Genuine holiness (spirituality) leads to service. When in the spring of 1855 Dominic Savio opened his heart to Don Bosco and manifested his yearning to become a saint, he was told to make efforts to do good to his classmates. This apostolic activity was practiced constantly by men and women desirous of growing in the spiritual life. True love of God is proven by love for one's neighbor. The growing commitment of today's young people to be of service springs from their personal love for Christ, coupled with a desire to make Him known and loved. New fields of service are opening for youth. "Love for life, as a sign of the Spirit in Don Bosco's style, can find adequate ways for employing the best energies of the world of youth."[15]

There can be no authentic education unless talents and aptitudes are brought to full maturity by helping youth seek the moral development and growth of their peers. They are educated for a life of dialogue and service. The World Youth rallies have been the Holy Father's invitation to youth to renew spiritual values in themselves first and then to make the gospel values better known and appreciated by their peers. Youth encounters become means of personal growth, ways to deepen youth's sense of belonging to the Church, leading them to encounter Christ in apostolic commitments. There is a continuous effort today to promote youth movements characterized by Salesian spirituality. We have already spoken of the Merry Company established by Don Bosco during his student days at Chieri. Today we have St. Dominic Savio Clubs, TEC (Teens Encounter Christ), Antioch weekends, and a host of different parish activities geared to youth.

In Salesian schools, much emphasis is placed on personal witness of the educators themselves to create a genuinely religious atmosphere. "The witness of faith of the educators influences the environment and creates a school culture that especially impacts the more mature students, who in turn become the joyful daily leaven for a growth in youth spirituality among their peers."[16]

Models

I would like to close this chapter by sketching two historical figures: first, a fifteen-year-old boy, Dominic Savio, who risked his life to help victims of cholera; second, the tragic story of a thirteen-year-old girl, Laura Vicuña, who offered her life for her mother. Both were the products of Salesian education.

■ **Dominic Savio.** In late October 1854, Dominic Savio entered Don Bosco's Oratory in Turin. He was accepted into this boarding school, which lodged one hundred fifteen boys from all classes of society. He endured with equanimity the poor accommodations, scarcity of food, and lack of heat during the winter months. Above all, he had to bear with some rough companions.

The gentle care and loving kindness of Don Bosco and his young Salesians made it all worthwhile. The life of prayer and study and play were all a great help to mold his character and deepen his faith. Grateful for having been accepted by Don Bosco, Dominic was very supportive of what the young Salesians were hoping to achieve. In his own unobtrusive way he began, little by little, to gain ascendancy over his peers, and he had a stabilizing effect on them. On one occasion, Dominic broke up a fight between two of the older boys who had been at odds for a long time. The conflict led to a stone-throwing duel to determine who was right or wrong. Upon learning of this struggle, Dominic went to the site of the duel. When both boys had distanced themselves and were ready to start throwing stones, Dominic placed himself in the middle. With a crucifix in his hand, he recalled to the whole crowd how Christ died forgiving all his enemies. The two boys, impressed by Savio's action and words, threw down their stones and peace was restored. The bystanders were awed.

Don Bosco, always forgetful of self, made constant sacrifices to shelter and feed his boys, whose number continued to increase. They followed his example. In the early part of the year 1854, cholera broke out in Turin and thousands perished. The mayor of the city called for volunteers to help the plague-stricken. Don Bosco rallied his boys and went to the aid of the unfortunate ones. Mamma Margaret gave the boys altar cloths to use for sheets and bandages. She even sacrificed her own wedding dress. Later in the same year, cholera broke out again. The Oratory boys followed Don Bosco into the garrets and hovels searching for victims. This time Dominic Savio, recently admitted to the Oratory, joined the generous volunteers.

In the Oratory there reigned a family atmosphere marked by cordiality, peace, and joy. This atmosphere was the result of duty well done. Don Bosco's educational philosophy placed great emphasis on personal responsibility, study, prayer life, recreation, suffering heat and cold, putting up with others, peer ministry, social action. Dominic was generous in assisting the sick, teaching catechism, helping others with their schoolwork. This attitude explains why one day he remarked to a homesick boy, "Here, we make holiness consist in always being very cheerful." Some might say that this remark was naive. Observers and admirers find the same formula in all Salesian centers throughout the world. Its basis rests on Don Bosco's often repeated advice: "Try to avoid sin, which is the great enemy that can steal from us God's grace and peace of heart. Then we try to be faithful to our duties."

■ **Laura Vicuña.** In the history of the early Church, we are impressed by accounts of young virgins who died for the faith while defending their chastity. Familiar names like Agnes, Agatha, Cecilia, and Rosalia remain models of fidelity and integrity. Closer to our own times, we witness the growing devotion to St. Maria Goretti who died because of multiple wounds inflicted by a would-be rapist whose advances she resisted. Today she remains a model of purity in a world beset with sexual freedom and promiscuity.

From another part of the world, at the foot of the Andes, comes a tragic story of wounds inflicted on a young girl, Laura Vicuña, who died at the age of thirteen. As she was dying, she confided to her mother in a weak voice: "Mama, I am dying. It is something I myself asked of Jesus. Nearly two years ago I offered my life for your salvation, that you would be given the grace to return to God. Won't you give me the joy of seeing you repent before I die?" The mother, overcome with remorse, answered: "O Laura, my child, I swear here and now that I will do what you ask of me. I do repent and God is the witness of this promise that I make."[17]

Laura was born on April 5, 1891, in Santiago, Chile. She was the first child of Domenico Vicuña and Mercedes Pino. Her father's family, one of the leading families of Chile, was involved in the revolution taking place at that time. With his wife and daughter, Domenico fled to Temuco, where he was killed in 1893. Shortly afterwards, Doña Mercedes left Chile for Argentina with her two daughters Laura and little Julia, who had been born after her father's death. Mercedes became involved with a wealthy rancher, Manuel Mora. In June 1900 the mother placed both children in a boarding school at the foot of the mountains in Junín de los Andes, Argentina. This school was conducted by the Salesian Sisters.

Laura was happy in her new environment under the kind and gentle care of the Sisters, who followed the Salesian educational method of reason, religion, kindness. Laura matured spiritually, intellectually, socially, and emotionally. Like Dominic Savio, she was generous with her classmates and forgetful of herself. She excelled in sports. Under the care of the chaplain and the Sisters, she developed a love for prayer and became an active member of the peer ministry group called the Children of Mary.

In June, 1901, Laura made her First Communion, an occasion of great happiness. Yet it was a day of sorrow because her mother was not able to join her at the altar on account of her lifestyle. Laura determined to pray and sacrifice for her mother's conversion. In her resolutions on this day, she promised the Lord to make reparation for the offenses received from people, especially from those in her family.

In January of 1902, Laura and her sister, Julia, went to spend the summer with their mother. The rancher, Manuel Mora, began to show undue attention to the young woman, Laura, who was careful to avoid him. When the children returned to school, the Sisters received them even though they could not pay the tuition since the rancher refused to pay. At school, Laura approached the school chaplain who allowed her to make a private vow. She intensified her prayers for her mother. At the end of 1902, Laura suffered a physical breakdown and her condition deteriorated in the following month. Her mother went to Junín de los Andes to get her daughter medical help. Here she rented rooms, as her daughter would not live under the same roof with Manuel. When he came to visit, Laura threatened to return to school if he remained overnight. When she tried to go back to school, the rancher went after her and struck her mercilessly and left her half dead on the road. Her mother took her to the hospital where she died after revealing to her mother that she had offered her life for her conversion. Laura received with joy her mother's promise to change her way of life. On January 22, 1904, Laura went to her eternal reward. Like Maria Goretti, who chose death rather than commit sin, Laura preferred death to acquiescence in evil. Her mother, Mercedes, kept her word and remained faithful to her promise till her death in 1929. Pope John Paul, on the occasion of the centennial of the death of St. John Bosco, declared Laura Blessed and spoke these memorable words: "The new Blessed whom we honor today is a special product of the education she received from the Daughters of Mary, Help of Christians, and is therefore a significant part of the heritage of Don Bosco. It is right, therefore, to turn our thoughts to the Institute of the Salesian Sisters and their foundress in order to obtain deeper devotion to their founders and new apostolic zeal particularly in the Christian formation of youth."[18]

Behold Your Mother

This chapter would be incomplete if I did not add a section on Mary, the Mother of God, Mother of the Church, Help of Christians, and Mother of Youth! You might be surprised that I should use the expression *Mother of Youth,* but I would say, And why not? Let's discuss the role of Mary in adolescent life.

I already mentioned the letter written by Pope John Paul on the occasion of the 1988 centennial anniversary of the death of St. John Bosco; the *Father and Teacher of Youth* had a tender devotion to Mary, the Lady of his first dream and the beacon of his apostolic mission. The Pope concludes his letter with an appeal to the members of the Salesian Family to look always to Mary:

> Keep always before you Mary, most Holy, the most lofty collaborator of the Holy Spirit, who was docile to his inspirations and so became the Mother of Christ and Mother of the Church. She continues through the centuries to be a maternal presence as is shown by Christ's words spoken from the Cross: "Woman, behold your son; behold your Mother."
>
> Never take your gaze off Mary: listen to her when she says "Do whatever He tells you." Pray to her too with daily solicitude, that the Lord may continue to raise up generous souls who can say "yes" to His vocational call. To her I entrust you, and with you the whole world of youth, that being attracted, animated, and guided by her, they may be able to attain through the mediation of your educative work, the stature of new men and women for a new world: the world of Christ, Master and Lord.[19]

The Holy Father entrusted the Salesian Family and the world of youth to Mary.

Following the example of Don Bosco, who always kept his gaze on Mary, the members of the Salesian Family do the same and invite the young to focus on Mary, the Help of Christians. They make their own Don Bosco's words to the young, when he produced his first prayer book and called it *The Companion of Youth*. In the section on Mary, he wrote:

> A great help to you, my friends, is devotion to the Blessed Virgin Mary who invites all with these words of welcome "Whoever are little, let them come to me." If you are devoted to her, she will shower abundant blessings upon you in this life, with a guarantee of life in heaven.... Be persuaded that you will receive every grace from this good Mother, provided that what you ask is for the good of your soul.... Above all, seek three graces: flight from mortal sin, love for chastity, and avoidance of bad company. With these three graces you will continue on your journey of faith on the road which will make you good members of society, and you will have the secure guarantee of eternal happiness, which Mary obtains for all her children.[20]

In Mary, Don Bosco is pointing out to the young the source of their ability to become "good Christians and useful citizens."

There is no question that Don Bosco's mother instilled devotion in him at a very early age. We already mentioned that on leaving for the seminary (1830), John received the recommendation: "Love those who love Mary; if some day you become a priest, constantly promote devotion to her." He constantly expressed his devotion to Mary; no sacrifice was too great for him to show honor to the Mother of God. In 1864, though penniless, he launched the building of a great Basilica in Turin in honor of Mary. In 1872 he founded a new congregation of Sisters whom he called Daughters of Mary, Help of Christians; they were to be a living monument of gratitude for all that Mary had done to further his mission on behalf of youth. In 1884, in Rome, he was interviewed by a reporter from the Paris newspaper *Le Monde*. Asked how he was able to build institutions and churches and to send missionary expeditions overseas, Don Bosco answered simply, "The secret of all my resources is Mary, Help of Christians."

Devotion to Mary was one of the three devotions that Don Bosco left in heritage to his spiritual sons and daughters. There is no doubt that they have been faithful to his wish, especially in encouraging this devotion to all and in particular to the young. On his deathbed, Don Bosco told those around him: "Tell my friends that I shall be waiting for them in Paradise." He had already told them that devotion to Mary was the surest guarantee of gaining heaven.

CHAPTER 6

1. Mark 10:13–16.
2. Bosco, *Memoirs of the Oratory of St. Francis de Sales,* 18.
3. *Vatican Council II,* no. 1, 726–727.
4. Pope John Paul II, "*Juvenum Patris,*" no. 8, 20–21.
5. Ibid., no. 16, 30–31.

6. Paul Aronica, *St. Dominic Savio* (New Rochelle, NY: Don Bosco Publications, 1979), 49–50.
7. Pope Pius XI, *Seven Great Encyclicals,* 65.
8. *Constitutions of the Daughters of Mary, Help of Christians* (Rome, Italy: Institute of the Daughters of Mary, Help of Christians, 1982), c. 5, 29–31.
9. *Constitutions and Regulations of the Society of St. Francis de Sales,* 1984, c. 25, 31, c. 34, 40.
10. *Constitutions and Regulations of the Society of St. Francis de Sales,* 1949, 45.
11. Cf. Salesians of Don Bosco, *XXIII General Chapter,* Rome: Italy, 1990, 103.
12. Cf. Lemoyne, *Biographical Memoirs,* 5: 135.
13. *Constitutions and Regulations of the Society of St. Francis de Sales,* 1984, c. 34, 40.
14. Salesians of Don Bosco, *XVIII General Chapter,* 110.
15. Ibid., 115.
16. *Acts of the General Council,* no. 344 (Rome, Italy: Direzione Generale Opere Don Bosco, 1993), 37.
17. Peter Lappin, *The Falcon and the Dove* (New Rochelle, NY: Don Bosco Publications, 1984), 150.
18. *L'Osservatore Romano* (Vatican City, Rome, Italy) 26 September 1988, 14.
19. Pope John Paul II, "*Juvenum Patris,*" no. 20, 35.
20. John Bosco, *The Companion of Youth* (Battersea, London; England: The Salesian Press, 1955), 22–24.

7 Kindness: Reaching the Hearts of the Young

Upon hearing of *Boys Town,* the older generation thinks of the Spencer Tracy movie. Not everyone knows that the founder of this well-known institution was Fr. Edward Joseph Flanagan (1886–1948). Two years after his ordination (1912), with no formal training, he began a hotel for derelict men in downtown Omaha, Nebraska. He soon became convinced that rehabilitation must begin early, during the impressionable years of adolescence: An ounce of prevention is worth a pound of cure! He also understood that the environment has an important part to play in the education of the young. In 1917, he gave up the hotel and bought two temporary homes for teenagers. In 1922, he purchased the Overlook Farm, ten miles from Omaha; it was here that he founded Boys Town.[1]

If we go farther back in history, we will meet another newly ordained priest moved with the same compassion for the poor and abandoned. He began his work in the city of Turin, Italy, in the early stages of the Industrial Revolution in a divided country undergoing political upheaval. Waves of migration to the city from the country-side brought thousands of young people in search of work and security and a place to live. The local government was too concerned with the struggle for independence from foreign rulers to attend to the needs of these uprooted youths. Delinquency was rampant. The zealous priest who came on the scene was Don Bosco. It was the fall of 1841!

An Ounce of Prevention

Turin was to be the place for his apostolic work—a prophetic dream/vision led the way to this city in northwestern Italy. He would later be known as the Apostle of Turin, as his model and inspiration, St. Philip Neri, was already known as the Apostle of Rome. The pioneering work of both saints continues through the Congregations that they founded.

Don Bosco was also encouraged to come to Turin by his spiritual director, St. Joseph Cafasso, who together with another zealous priest conducted a graduate school of theology for young priests. The two-year course was to train these priests in pastoral preaching and in the defense of the Church's teachings. Training did not remain on an abstract and theoretical level. All students were required to be involved in ministry in the city parishes. Their service included the sacramental life, the care of the sick, and visits to prisons. A priority was to give religious instruction to all and in particular, to the young. Some priests were to become chaplains in the local prisons and youth detention centers. Don Bosco was encouraged to go to the prisons to minister to the inmates. He also came in contact with those condemned to the gallows. His first experience standing on the platform with the condemned was memorable. He fainted! That was the end of that particular ministry. This experience revealed the delicate and sensitive soul of Don Bosco.

His visits to the prisons continued for a while. He witnessed appalling conditions. What especially pained him was to see youngsters thrown in with hardened criminals. For petty thievery and other minor infractions of the law, boys were locked up with men who had led a life of crime. There was no chance for rehabilitation! On returning from such visits, Don Bosco was distraught. He gave time to prayer and discernment. Something had to be done. The only road to follow was that of prevention. Someone had to care for these young people and help educate them so that they could become *good Christians and useful citizens.* What was uppermost in the mind of this young priest was the need to create a healthy moral environment where the development of the whole person could occur. Don Bosco believed in the basic goodness of human nature, he left this outlook to all his followers. "Inspired by the optimistic St. Francis de Sales, [the Salesian] believes in man's natural humanism and supernatural resources without losing sight of his weakness. He is able to make his own what is good in the world and does not bewail his own times; he accepts all that is good, especially if it appeals to the young."[2]

Free from destructive influences and poor living conditions, youth could succeed in finding a place in society. Given a chance, the young can mature into *good Christians and useful citizens*. Years later, Fr. Flanagan would coin his famous expression: "There is no such thing as a bad boy!"

Love Conquers All

Throughout his life Don Bosco wanted to be sure that he was doing the will of God. After prayer and reflection, he would seek the counsel of his mentor, Fr. Joseph Cafasso, who had followed John through his early years. In fact it was this wise priest who advised John to go to the seminary and become a diocesan priest rather than enter a religious order. With the approval and blessing of his spiritual director, John entered his field of apostolic activity on behalf of poor and abandoned youth.

After spending a third year of further study and preparation for his new mission, Don Bosco entered a new stage of his life. A number of questions suggest themselves. What did he bring to this new venture? What experiences had shaped his mind and heart? In addition to knowledge acquired through books and the theories of others, did he have his own personal experience? Did he have a story that shaped him for the historical role that he was to play in society as a founder and educator with a philosophy of his own? The answer to these questions is Yes!

This is how John tells his own story:

> I was not yet two when my father died, and I no longer remember what he looked like. The earliest recollection I have in my life is that my mother said to me: "Now you have no father!"

Everyone left my father's room, but I insisted on staying. My mother sorrowfully told me: "Come, John, come with me, you no longer have a father!" I answered: "If papa doesn't come, I won't come either." Thereupon, she broke into sobs, took my hand and led me away. Because she was crying I burst into tears myself. At that age I certainly did not understand what a great loss it was to lose one's father. But, I have always remembered those words: "Now you have no father!" I still remember what we did to comfort my brother Anthony, who was beside himself with grief. I don't remember anything else from that day until I was four or five.[3]

    I specifically mention this incident because it seems to me that this loss was somehow compensated for, consciously and unconsciously, by the extraordinary love he had for youth throughout his life. He died at the age of seventy-two, and his death was attributed to physical exhaustion and bodily deterioration—the result of having spent himself on behalf of the young: begging for their needs; opening academic and vocational schools; recruiting followers, men and women, to continue his work for the moral and human regeneration of thousands of abandoned young people.

    The secret of his success was love and charity and kindness. He chose a text of St. Paul as the foundation of his philosophy: The practice of this system is wholly based on the words of St. Paul who says: "Love is patient and kind . . . Love bears all things, hopes all things, endures all things" (1 Cor 13: 4–7). Scattered throughout the writings of this nineteenth-century educator we find expressions such as: "Education is a matter of the heart . . . friendly counsel which appeals to the heart of the young and wins over the heart . . . the educator will speak in the language of the heart . . . I will do all I can if only I can win the hearts of the young. . . . After winning the heart of a pupil, the educator can exercise great influence over that person. . . . Let us make ourselves loved, and we shall possess their hearts."

It is interesting to note that when a biblical passage was sought for the entrance prayer for the Liturgy celebrated on the Feast of St. John Bosco (January 31), the words were taken from the first Book of Kings, words that referred to King Solomon: "God gave him wisdom and understanding and a *heart* as vast as the sands on the seashore." In his treatise on the *preventive system,* Don Bosco makes reference to a striking analogy used by St. Gregory to describe the role kindness and love play in winning the human heart. Only moral strength can win the human heart, which St. Gregory tells us is like an impregnable fortress, never to be conquered except by affection and kindness.[4]

Don Bosco made every effort to reach the heart. The secret of his success was there. He was convinced through personal experience that after winning the heart of the young, the educator can exercise great influence even later in life. He encouraged those having difficulty winning over a difficult youngster to seek the help of one who can more easily win over his heart. It would seem at times that a teenager reaps no profit from corrections, yet deep in his heart there is a gradual change taking place.

Psychology and Love

Karl Menninger in his insightful book *Whatever Became of Sin?* illustrates the deep value of love in the healing process of mentally ill patients. One day in his famed hospital, the Menninger Institute in Topeka, Kansas, he carried out an experiment. Calling the entire staff from all levels of service (from doctors and nurses to cooks and janitors), he told them of his conviction that the time spent in the mental hospital could be significantly reduced. How? Simply by going about one's duties with a great deal of genuine love and joyful caring and gentle affirmation. This loving attitude was to be exercised by all, even the employees cleaning the rooms and changing the light bulbs. To the surprise and satisfaction of the entire staff, the time patients were hospitalized was significantly reduced.[5]

It is also reported that Dr. Menninger asked his resident students to identify the most important part of the treatment process of mental patients. Some said it was the relationship between the therapist and the patient; others thought it was a list of recommendations; still others spoke of the necessity of contact with the families after a patient was discharged; a group thought it was the prescription of drugs. However, Menninger did not accept any of these suggestions; for him the first and foremost task of any healer or therapist was *to listen:* "After decades of work as a psychiatrist, Menninger believed that the experience of not being listened to made people unwell, and the experience of being listened to made them well again. The experience of stillness in the presence of another person gave them a sense of their God-given purpose in life. . . . Listening to someone may not seem like much, but its effects are very healing. Everyone yearns to be heard."[6]

The author himself recalls a personal experience. In the many counseling classes he attended, he frequently heard the expression *to listen with the third ear.* The professor (a psychiatrist) was emphasizing the importance of attentive listening that can hear what is not being said. The secret to this listening is observation: observation of body language, choice of words, tone of voice, facial expressions. To be able to intuit problems is satisfying both for the therapist and for the client. The same dynamics are in play when an adult is truly present and listening to a troubled youth.

Hope Not Hopelessness

In his adolescent years and later, Don Bosco had many reasons to give into discouragement: growing up in a one-parent family and disfunctional at that (his stepbrother thwarted every effort made to let John attend school). Poverty was his constant companion; and because of the dire needs of his family, he was forced to work in the fields at a very early age. When he was finally able to go to school, he had to find odd jobs to help pay his tuition and board. Even in the seminary he earned money for various services to his fellow seminarians and thus was able to meet his financial obligations. Winning the top scholastic award each year was another way to obtain extra money. In all these difficult situations, he did not lose heart! The virtue of hope was his strength and the ground of his perseverance. In the Liturgy of the Mass in honor of St. John Bosco the words aptly chosen for the Communion prayer were those applied to the patriarch Abraham. He was promised by God that he would become the father of many nations . . . and he was commanded to offer in sacrifice his son Isaac. His obedience was rewarded, and his son was spared. Don Bosco, though tried in many ways, remained faithful. Sustained by the virtue of hope, he became the Father and Teacher of endless numbers of youth who found and continue to find warmth and love and shelter and hope in the thousands of Salesian centers conducted by his Sons and Daughters.

From his own experience, he knew how to cultivate this hope in the young who came to him. He imbued his followers with the same hope; this attitude was crystallized in Constitution 63 of the Salesians: ". . . [this consecration] makes the Salesian a sign of the power of the Resurrection . . . fashions his heart entirely for the kingdom, helps him to discern and welcome God's action in history. In the simplicity and hard work of daily life they transform him into an educator who proclaims to the young 'new heavens and a new earth,' awakening in them hope and the dedication and joy to which it gives rise."[7]

Among the many problems facing youth today, we find a sense of hopelessness at the top of the list. Many young people, poor and abandoned, do not see a way out of hellish poverty and impossible home conditions. They need someone who cares and takes a direct interest in them and helps them believe that there is a light at the end of the tunnel, if only they will continue forward on their journey. Federal, state, and local agencies are definitely necessary. Are they enough? No! I do not think so. Coordinators, leaders, and supervisors must be men and women who care, who love, who will go the extra mile. The many charitable agencies of different religious groups are shining examples of what can be done by so many dedicated and loving volunteers.

Personal interest and constant dedication must go beyond professional obligations if we are to fulfill the basic needs of youth, through love, acceptance, recognition, and affirmation. Among the cries of youth we hear the following: "We need things to do, places to visit, people to be with. Give us healthy experiences so we stay away from drugs, sex, and violence." A director of a youth program in a big city put it this way: "Teenagers would get into less trouble if adults spent more time with them. I don't believe it's guns or drugs or violence that's the problem. I believe kids are being neglected. Our kids are not demonic." It all sounds like Fr. Flanagan all over again: "There is no such thing as a bad boy." Or as Don Bosco put it: "Though I have been dealing with boys for forty years, I do not recall having used punishments of any kind; and yet by the help of God I have always obtained not only what duty required, but also what was simply a wish on my part, and that from the very boys in regard to whom all hope of success seemed lost."[8]

Caring and Nurturing Environment

The Friend of Youth, Don Bosco, exemplified the meaning of teacher and leader of youth in his writings and, above all, in practicing what he preached. The environment he created and urged his followers to maintain was not cold and correct but warm and inviting. This was and is a crucial element in his method of education. Experienced principals and teachers know this very well and work at it. Seasoned educators sense whether or not such an environment exists, as they enter a school or classroom or youth club.

An inner-city principal made it a point to remind the school staff frequently of the importance of not separating the heart from the head. This is a constant in terms of discipline. How principals and teachers relate to the students is crucial to how learning takes place. This principal said: "We become their [the pupils'] focal point of security during the day. And if they know they are loved, they can do anything." Of course, to be a principal in an inner-city school, you have to be motivated and a real spiritual person. You cannot do this without saying, "I've got to trust in God that it's going to work out." Someone else put it this way, speaking of the office of a principal: "What an awesome responsibility: demanding, frustrating, but it's wonderful!"

Not enough can be said about the importance of the environment! In Salesian literature we find an abundant emphasis on the environment, which channels education as if by osmosis: values and virtues, ideals and ideas, maxims and morals. True education always teaches in one way or another, provided all the school personnel (administration, teachers, and all ancillary staff) have in mind the good of the students. The environment is a valuable teacher. The effects of such an atmosphere are imperceptible, but they are nonetheless real and lasting. G. K. Chesterton put it well: "Every education teaches a philosophy, if not by dogma, then by suggestion, by implication, by atmosphere. Every part of that education has a connection with every other part. If it does not all combine to convey some general view of life, it is not education at all!"[9]

Don Bosco made every effort to create an environment where the family spirit reigned; he achieved this through rapport, friendliness, presence, respect, attention, dedication to service, and personal responsibility. Not only did he teach this, but he exemplified it through his own actions. He became an inspiration to his followers, who were sent to open youth centers and schools all over the globe. His parting words were always: "Do as you saw done at the Oratory!" His words were both inspiration and motivation. Today we find many educators speaking the same language, insisting on forming a school community. A successful modern educator, Dr. Thomas J. Sergiovanni, begins his book *Building Community in Schools* with these striking words:

> The story I tell in *Building Community in Schools* is a simple one. Though most principals, superintendents, and teachers have a desire to do better and are working as hard as they can to provide a quality education to every student they serve, the road is rough and the going slow. The lead villain in this frustrating drama is the loss of community in our schools and in society itself. If we want to rewrite the script to enable good schools to flourish, we need to rebuild community. Community building must become the heart of any school improvement effort. Whatever else is involved—improving teaching, developing sensible curriculum, creating new forms of governance, providing more authentic assessment, empowering teachers and parents, increasing professionalism—it must rest on a foundation of community building.[10]

CHAPTER 7

1. *New Catholic Encyclopedia,* "Flanagan, Edward Joseph" (New York: McGraw-Hill Book Company, 1967), 5: 357.
2. *Constitutions and Regulations of the Society of St. Francis de Sales,* 1984, c. 17.
3. Cf. Bosco, *Memoirs of the Oratory of St. Francis de Sales,* 7–8.
4. Cf. Lemoyne, "The Use of Punishments in Salesian Houses," *Biographical Memoirs,* 16: 369.
5. Karl Menninger, *Whatever Became of Sin* (New York: Hawthorn Books. 1973).
6. Thomas J. Morgan, *The Heart of Ministry, Human Development,* XV, no. 4 (winter 1994) 35.

7. *Constitutions and Regulations of the Society of St. Francis de Sales,* 1984, c. 63, 59.
8. Ibid., 253.
9. G. K. Chesterton, *The Common Man,* as quoted by Fr. Leonard Foley, O.F.M. in *Saints of the Day,* (Cincinnati: St. Anthony Messenger Press, 1974), vol. I (January 31), 34.
10. Thomas J. Sergiovanni, *Building Community in Schools* (San Francisco: Jossey-Bass Publishers, 1994), xi.

Conclusion: Don Bosco's Contribution to Education

Don Bosco's story can be called a success story because he substantially enriched the theory and practice of human and Christian education. From my own perspective, I present the following conclusions, while leaving it to others to enrich us with their insights

■ **An educator in action.** Don Bosco was not a theoretician in matters of pedagogy; rather he was a *practitioner*. We do not have a large quantity of written educational material from his hand; in a few seminal documents (see Appendixes A, B, and C) and in other writings, we find nuggets of wisdom and practical advice for those engaged in the difficult art of educating the young, whether in group settings or one-to-one. Don Bosco left us himself as a model and thereby provided us with a variety of practical norms and concrete guidelines that are of priceless value to those involved in the challenging task of guiding youth. His biography, written by those who knew him firsthand, fills nineteen volumes. It is a treasury of educational and counseling techniques. He did indeed teach others how to be educators; but more importantly, he demonstrated his principles in concrete situations as an educator and youth counselor. Don Bosco will always remain a model of the educator in action.

■ **Christian education revitalized.** Our saint did not create a new system, but rather followed the best that was to be found in traditional Christian education. He then took the positive elements in the psychology of his day and applied a Christian humanistic approach to the formation and development of the character of the young. His distinctive contribution, therefore, lies in the fact that he was able to revive an almost forgotten method—that of the message of love found in the Gospel. By so doing, he not only rekindled a smoldering fire, but also crystallized the *preventive* approach into definite memorials, both written and living. The written memorial was his manual outlining the Salesian way (see Appendix A). The living memorials are the members of his Salesian Family, who are guided by his system.

■ **Youth activities and organizations.** Don Bosco was a prime mover and a daring forerunner in the organization of various activities for the young. In his day it was unheard of for a priest to place himself in such a position. This innovation brought him ridicule and contempt on the part of the clergy and suspicion and annoyance on the part of civil authorities who feared this "radical" priest herding a large band of deprived teenagers! Fear of some sort of confrontation clouded their minds, and the good he accomplished was overlooked. Today, his innovation is taken for granted. Youth organizations and activities are recognized as an integral part of education. Such involvement is considered essential in the development of physical and mental hygiene, as well as in the formation of character, social growth, and working together.

■ **Civic responsibility.** Don Bosco likewise encouraged teenagers to develop and foster within themselves a concern for community and society. He was concerned that youth play its part to build bridges, not walls, for the betterment of all. His plan called for youth involvement; he personally demonstrated his care when in 1854 he volunteered himself and invited his boys to help during the cholera epidemic that swept through the city twice that year, claiming many victims. On other occasions his youthful friends took the lead in organizing events for the benefit of the neediest students. Their leadership qualities were not so much taught but caught from the master, Don Bosco.

■ **Friendly relationships.** In the period of history during which Don Bosco lived, there was a great psychological distance between teacher and pupil. This gap facilitated stern discipline, but it was also a barrier that prevented the personal contact and friendly relationships that are so necessary in the process of education. Our saint restored to educators an awareness that rapport and kindness are vital for security, warmth, and closeness on which the process of maturation depends. Knowing from experience that mutual understanding and sincere friendliness are the key to success in any educational endeavor, Don Bosco called all teachers to the practice of gentleness, amiability, and meekness. His efforts in this field won for him the title "Blessed Friend of Youth." He called teachers back to the imitation of the greatest of all teachers, Christ, who loved to repeat that he was meek and humble of heart.

This demonstration of the role of kindness will ever remain Don Bosco's outstanding contribution. An eminent educator has spoken of Don Bosco's system as the humanization of discipline. The very name "Salesian" that Don Bosco chose for his religious and lay followers was a reference to St. Francis de Sales (1567–1622), the "gentleman saint" of sixteenth-century France.

■ **Moral and religious training.** A number of public school educators today are asking that some type of moral teaching be restored to our nation's schools. Their motive is apparent when we observe all around us the evils of permissiveness, drugs, violence, and a total disregard for law and order and standards of morality. As long as we keep God out of our schools, we are depriving our young people of a system of values that will benefit them individually and society collectively. While busy seeking jobs and housing for his boys, Don Bosco did not stop there but strove to solve moral and social problems. He immediately put the emphasis where it belonged—on religion. He could not conceive of an "amoral education"; the three Rs could have no meaning without the presence of the fourth R, religion.

Conclusion

The desire of many modern educators to restore moral teaching to our classrooms is a recognition that an education with lasting effects must rest on the secure basis of religion. Don Bosco insisted that moral and religious education rest on the frequent use of three spiritual props: 1) the sacraments of reconciliation (confession) and the Eucharist; 2) devotion to the Mother of God, Mary Immaculate; and 3) the need for the constant guidance and light of the Church in the person of the Holy Father. Fidelity to our faith and regular Church attendance make available the liturgical life and the means of grace that bring peace to the heart. In religious practice, men and women enjoy an ethical guide to the meaning of life.

■ **An ounce of prevention.** We know the plight of young people in our large cities. They are getting into all sorts of trouble. The situation is a cause of deep concern for those in authority. It was because of a somewhat similar situation that Don Bosco began his work for the young people who were roaming the streets of Turin; they had nothing to do, nowhere to go. The result was that they ended up in trouble with the law. How could such a situation be prevented?

Don Bosco brought to education a realization of the need for prevention of wrongdoing through active fatherly (or brotherly) supervision. Personal participation in the activities of youth affords the teacher and educator an opportunity for counsel and guidance. These elements of supervision, counsel, and guidance are preventive techniques that in Don Bosco's system obviate most corrective punishment (see Appendix B).

■ **Presence and rapport.** Don Bosco, fearing that his spiritual sons might be losing sight of the Salesian spirit that he worked so hard to develop and instill in them, tried to impress upon them the need for greater availability and personal contact on a one-to-one basis when dealing with teenagers. In the letter of 1884 from Rome (see Appendix C), he lamented the fact that his Salesians were not mingling with the young as they did before, and this created a barrier. "As I looked there were very few Salesians with the youngsters . . . they were no longer the heart and soul of their activities . . . some Salesians did not want to mingle with the boys, who began to break away from them . . . the present change in the Oratory [Don Bosco's first school] was due to a lack of confidence in the Salesians on the part of the boys." All this was due to the lack of personal contact with the young. Don Bosco reminded his sons that this barrier could be broken down "by a friendly relationship. . . . Affection cannot be shown without this friendly relationship . . . he who wants to be loved must first show his own love." Finally, Don Bosco reminded the Salesians of the importance for continuing kindness and charity: "Let us all be at one in this: let the charity of those who are in authority and the charity of those who have to obey cause the spirit of St. Francis de Sales to reign among us." He wanted them never to forget the three key words of his *preventive* approach to education: Reason, Religion, Kindness—keys that would enable them to reach out and unlock the hearts of youth.

■ **Mary, our Mother.** In Chapter 6, "Religion: Walking the Journey of Faith with the Young," we spoke of Mary, the Mother of God, and we gave her the title *Mother of Youth*. Salesian educators, following the example of their founder, St. John Bosco, continue to foster and encourage youth to cultivate devotion to Mary. Pope John Paul, in his letter of 1988, wrote, to the Salesians: "To her I entrust you, and with you the whole world of youth, that being attracted, animated and guided by her, they may be able to attain through the meditation of your educative work, the stature of new men for a new world: the world of Christ, Master and Lord."[1]

Don Bosco had a tender and warm devotion to Mary; it had its human foundation in his deep relationship with his own mother, widowed when John was two years of age. It was natural

Conclusion

and psychologically healthy for him to transfer this relationship to Mary, the Mother of God, when John began to grow in his trust in Mary, the Lady of the first prophetic dream (1824). Mary played an important role in his life and mission. As far as the young were concerned, John emphasized that this devotion was vital in the life of the adolescent boy and girl. The breakdown of the family in today's society highlights the need for Mary. The lack of both or either parent leaves a deep void. This experience is especially sad when it is the mother who has left the family.

It will not be out of place to insert a story told by a professor at the Institute of Salesian Studies in Berkeley, California. The author was among his students:

> In 1955 the Salesians took on a challenge that many people considered risky and foolhardy. At the request of Milan's Archbishop Giovanni Montini (the future Pope Paul VI), the Salesians were asked to rescue a juvenile detention facility in the town of Arese (near Milan) that had become totally uncontrollable in the hands of its operators.
>
> When the Salesians took over the operation of the Beccaria Institute in Arese, they found graffiti everywhere—some quite shocking and obscene. But one very poignant scribble caught the eye of Fr. Della Torre, the newly appointed director. It read: 'SENZA UNA MAMMA, LA VITA NON HA SCOPO.' (Without a mother, life has no purpose.)[2]

This anecdote makes Don Bosco's assertion that Mary loves youth seem more relevant. She loves the young because she is a mother, and mothers have greater affection for the younger ones because they are more easily led astray and thus are more worthy of compassion. Don Bosco was well aware of the changes occurring in youth during the period of adolescence, their growing desire to break free from parental care and assert their independence. He realized that youth only too soon become aware of the fact that they are not psychologically and spiritually ready for the break, especially when it comes to solving new problems. "Adolescents are at an age at which they come to full stature and are quite willing and anxious to get along without help from anybody, but also at the age in which the souls discover their weakness. It is for their soul that the young want the help of a mother. True, one has his/her earthly mother, but a certain shame has come over them lately which prevents them from talking to their mothers about some very intimate things. They call on another mother, the mother of souls. The time has come for educators to point out to them Our Lady of Adolescents."[3]

In the first chapter we noted the great love that John Paul shows for all the young and the confidence he has in them. In several parts of this book we quoted him expressing admiration for St. John Bosco's pastoral and educational design. I wish to conclude this book with a statement that appeared in the Pope's recently published document *The Consecrated Life*. "The history of the Church, from antiquity down to our own day, is full of admirable examples of consecrated persons who have sought and continue to seek holiness through their involvement in education, while at the same time proposing holiness as the goal of education. Indeed, many of them have achieved the perfection of charity through teaching. This is one of the most precious gifts which consecrated persons today can offer to young people, instructing them in a way that is full of love, according to the wise counsel of Saint John Bosco: 'Young people should not only be loved but should also know that they are loved.'"[4]

CONCLUSION

1. Pope John Paul II, "*Juvenum Patris,*" no. 20: 35–38.
2. Michael Ribotta, Berkeley, CA., Institute of Salesian Studies, Intersession, 1995, Education 2125, 66. Classnotes given by M. Ribotta.
3. Robert Claude, *Training the Adolescent* (New York: Paulist Press, 1958), 44.
4. Pope John Paul II, *Consecrated Life* (Boston: Pauline Books & Media, 1996), 154.

SEMINAL DOCUMENTS
APPENDIXES A–C

Introduction

There is no better way to end this study of St. John Bosco's pastoral and educational plan than to present three of his writings that we call seminal. We use the word *seminal* because these documents contain the seeds of all of Don Bosco's teachings. Rich in principles and insights, they are the result of years of reflection and experience.

The first document, "The Preventive System in the Education of the Young" (Appendix A), was written in 1877, after thirty-six years of experience. The document is found in Vol. IV of the *English Biographical Memoirs,* EBM, (pp. 380–385). Its Italian original is found in Vol. XIII of *Memorie biografiche,* pp. 918–923. This writing is considered foundational in any study of Don Bosco—so much so that we find it in the Appendix to the Constitutions of the Salesians (pp. 246–253) and the Daughters of Mary, Help of Christians (pp. 433–441).

On January 29, 1883, Don Bosco wrote a special letter to all his followers on the subject of discipline and punishments. The prevailing practice of his day was repressive, and corporal punishments were common. He opposed this; he wanted his followers to do without any punishment if possible. Being a realist, he recognized that at times punishments had to be meted out. He then gave practical guidelines on when and how to punish. "The Use of Punishments in Salesian Houses" (Appendix B) covers this sensitive area. Its source is the recently published Vol. XVI of the *English Biographical Memoirs* (pp. 368–376).

The third document (Appendix C) is known as the "Letter from Rome—May 10, 1884." It is an appeal and a call to all Salesians to return to the original spirit of the Oratory. Two former students appear to Don Bosco in a dream and show him the way it was in the early days of his first center and how it had become. A copy of this document is to be found in the Appendix to the *Constitutions of the Society of St. Francis de Sales* (pp. 254–264) and of the *Constitutions of the Institute of the Daughters of Mary Help of Christians* (pp. 445–457). Its Italian original is to be found in *Memorie biografiche,* Vol. XVII (pp. 107–114), presently being translated. This letter was and still is an exhortation to preserve the heritage handed down to us.

A. The Preventive System in the Education of the Young[1]

On several occasions I have been asked to express verbally or in writing some thoughts about the so-called *preventive system,* which is in general use in our houses. Through lack of time I have so far been unable to meet these wishes; but as I now intend to print the rules of the houses, which until now have nearly always been used traditionally, I think it opportune to give a brief sketch, which may perhaps serve as an outline to a small book which I am preparing and hope to finish, if God gives me life enough, my sole purpose being to help in the difficult art of the education of the young. Wherefore I shall explain: in what the *preventive system* consists; why it ought to be preferred; and its practical application and its advantages.

1. In What the Preventive System Consists and Why It Should Be Preferred

There are two systems which have been in use through all ages in the education of youth: the *preventive* and the *repressive.* The *repressive system* consists in making the law known to the subjects, and afterwards watching to discover the transgressors of these laws, and inflicting, when necessary, the punishment deserved. According to this system, the words and looks of the superior must always be severe and even threatening, and he must avoid all familiarity with his dependents.

In order to give weight to his authority the Rector must rarely be found among his subjects, and as a rule only when it is a question of punishing or threatening. This system is easier, less troublesome, and especially suitable in the army and in general among adults and the judicious, who ought of themselves to know and remember what the law and regulations demand.

Quite different from this and I might even say opposed to it, is the *preventive system*. It consists in making the laws and regulations of an institute known, and then watching carefully so that the pupils may at all times be under the vigilant eye of the Rector or the assistants, who like loving fathers can converse with them, take the lead in every movement and in a kindly way give advice and correction; in other words, this system places the pupils in the impossibility of committing faults.

This system is based entirely on reason and religion, and above all on kindness; therefore it excludes all violent punishment, and tries to do without even the slightest chastisement. This system seems preferable for the following reasons:

1. Being forewarned the pupil does not lose courage on account of the faults he has committed, as is the case when they are brought to the notice of the superior. Nor does he resent the correction he receives or the punishment threatened or inflicted, because it is always accompanied by a friendly preventive warning, which appeals to his reason, and generally enlists his accord, so that he sees the necessity of the chastisement and almost desires it.

2. The primary reason for this system is the thoughtlessness of the young, who in one moment forget the rules of discipline and the penalties for their infringement. Consequently, a child often becomes culpable and deserving of punishment, which he had not even thought about, and which he had quite forgotten when heedlessly committing the fault he would certainly have avoided, had a friendly voice warned him.

3. The *repressive system* may stop a disorder, but can hardly make the offenders better. Experience teaches that the young do not easily forget the punishments they have received, and

for the most part foster bitter feelings, along with the desire to throw off the yoke and even to seek revenge. They may sometimes appear to be quite unaffected but anyone who follows them as they grow up knows that the reminiscences of youth are terrible; they easily forget punishments by their parents but only with great difficulty those inflicted by their teachers, and some have even been known in later years to have had recourse to brutal vengeance for chastisements they had justly deserved during the course of their education. In the *preventive system,* on the contrary, the pupil becomes a friend, and the assistant, a benefactor who advises him, has his good at heart, and wishes to spare him vexation, punishment, and perhaps dishonour.

4. By the *preventive system* pupils acquire a better understanding, so that an educator can always speak to them in the language of the heart, not only during the time of their education but even afterwards. Having once succeeded in gaining the confidence of his pupils he can subsequently exercise a great influence over them, and counsel them, advise and even correct them, whatever position they may occupy in the world later on.

2. Application of the Preventive System

The practice of this system is wholly based on the words of St Paul who says: *Caritas patiens est, benigna est. Omnia suffert, omnia sperat, omnia sustinet.*[2] "Love is patient and kind. . . . Love bears all things . . . hopes all things, endures all things." Hence only a Christian can apply the *preventive system* with success. Reason and religion are the means an educator must constantly apply; he must teach them and himself practice them, if he wishes to be obeyed and to attain his end.

1. It follows that the Rector must devote himself entirely to the boys; he should therefore never accept engagements which

might keep him from his duties, and he should always be with his pupils whenever they are not engaged in some occupation, unless they are already being properly supervised by others.

2. Teachers, craftmasters and assistants must be of acknowledged morality. They should strive to avoid as they would the plague every kind of affection or sentimental friendship for their pupils, and they should also remember that the wrongdoing of one alone is sufficient to compromise an educational institute. Care should be taken that the pupils are never alone. As far as possible the assistants ought to precede the boys to the place where they assemble; they should remain with them until others come to take their place, and never leave the pupils unoccupied.

3. Let the boys have full liberty to jump, run and make as much noise as they please. Gymnastics, music, theatricals and outings are most efficacious means of obtaining discipline and of benefiting spiritual and bodily health. Let care be taken however that the games, the persons playing them as well as the conversation are not reprehensible. *"Do anything you like,"* the great friend of youth, St. Philip [Neri], used to say, *"as long as you do not sin."*

4. Frequent confession and communion and daily Mass are the pillars which must support the edifice of education, from which we propose to banish the use of threats and the cane. Never force the boys to frequent the sacraments, but encourage them to do so, and give them every opportunity. On occasions of retreats, triduums, novenas, sermons and catechism classes let the beauty, grandeur and holiness of the Catholic religion be dwelt on, for in the sacraments it offers to all of us a very easy and useful means to attain our salvation and peace of heart. In this way children take readily to these practices of piety and will adopt them willingly with joy and benefit.

5. Let the greatest vigilance be exercised so as to prevent bad books, bad companions or persons who indulge in improper

Appendix A

conversations from entering the college. A good door-keeper is a treasure for a house of education.

6. Every evening after night prayers before the boys go to rest, the Rector or someone in his stead shall address them briefly, giving them advice or counsel concerning what is to be done or what is to be avoided. Let him try to draw some moral reflection from events that have happened during the day in the house or outside; but his words should never take more than two or three minutes. This is the key to good behavior, to the smooth running of the school and to success in education.

7. Avoid as a plague the opinion that the first communion should be deferred to a late age, when generally the Devil has already gained possession of a boy's heart, with incalculable prejudice to his innocence. According to the discipline of the early Church, it was the custom to give little children the consecrated hosts that remained over after the Easter communion. This serves to show us how much the Church desires children to be admitted to holy communion at an early age. When a child can distinguish between *Bread* and bread, and shows sufficient knowledge, give no further thought to his age, but let the heavenly King come and reign in that happy soul.

8. Catechisms invariably recommend frequent communion. St. Philip Neri counselled weekly and even more frequent communion. The Council of Trent clearly states that it greatly desires that every faithful Christian should receive holy communion whenever he hears Mass, and that this communion should not only be spiritual but also sacramental, so that greater fruit may be reaped from this august and divine sacrifice (*Conc. Trid.,* Sess. XXII, Chap. VI).

3. Advantages of the Preventive System

Some may say that this system is difficult in practice. I reply that for the pupils it is easier, more satisfactory and more advantageous. To the teacher it certainly does present some difficulties, which however can be diminished if he applies himself to his task with zeal. An educator is one who is consecrated to the welfare of his pupils, and therefore he should be ready to face every difficulty and fatigue in order to attain his object, which is the civic, moral and intellectual education of his pupils.

In addition to the advantages already mentioned, the following may be added:

1. The pupil will always be respectful towards his educators, and will ever remember their care with pleasure. He will look upon them as fathers and brothers. Wherever they may go, Salesian pupils are generally the consolation of their families, useful citizens and good Christians.

2. Whatever may be the character, disposition and moral state of a boy at the time of his admittance, parents can rest assured that their son will not become worse; indeed, it can be held as certain that he will always make some improvement. In fact, certain boys who for a long time had been the scourge of their parents, and had even been refused admittance to houses of correction, have changed their ways and habits when trained according to these principles, and begun to live upright lives, and are now filling honourable positions in society, and are the support of their families and a credit to the country they live in.

3. If it should happen that any boys who have already contracted bad habits enter the institute, they could not have a bad influence on their companions, nor would the good boys suffer any harm from association with them, since there is neither time, place nor opportunity, because the assistant, whom we suppose to be present, would speedily intervene.

4. A Word on Punishments

What rules should be followed in inflicting punishments? First of all never have recourse to punishments if possible, but when-

Appendix A

ever necessity demands stern measures, let the following be borne in mind:

1. An educator should seek to win the love of his pupils if he wishes to inspire fear in them. When he succeeds in doing this, the withholding of some token of kindness is a punishment which stimulates emulation, gives courage and never degrades.

2. With the young, punishment is whatever is meant as a punishment. It has been noticed that in the case of some boys a reproachful look is more effective than a slap in the face would be. Praise of work well done, and blame in the case of carelessness are already a reward or punishment.

3. Except in very rare cases, corrections and punishments should never be given publicly, but always privately and in the absence of companions; and the greatest prudence and patience should be used to bring the pupil to see his fault, with the aid of reason and religion.

4. To strike a boy in any way, to make him kneel in a painful position, to pull his ears, and other similar punishments, must be absolutely avoided, because the law forbids them, and because they greatly irritate the boys and degrade the educator.

5. The Rector shall make sure that the disciplinary measures, including rules and punishments, are known to the pupils, so that no one can make the excuse that he did not know what was commanded or forbidden.

If this system is carried out in our houses, I believe that we shall be able to obtain good results, without having recourse to the use of the cane and other corporal punishments. Though I have been dealing with boys for forty years, I do not recall having used punishments of any kind; and yet by the help of God I have always obtained not only what duty required, but also what was simply a wish on my part, and that from the very boys in regard to whom all hope of success seemed lost.

APPENDIX A

1. *Constitutions of the Society of St. Francis de Sales,* 1984, 246–253. Translated from "Regolamento per le case della Società di S. Francesco di Sales" (Torino, Italia, Tipografia Salesiana, 1877), 3–13; [OE XXIX, 99–109].
2. I Cor. 13:4, 7.

B The Use of Punishments in Salesian Houses[1]

Feast of St. Francis 1883

My dear sons,
Time and again, from various sources, I have been receiving requests, even pleas, to draw up some rules for our directors, headmasters, and teachers to guide them in the difficult cases when punishments are called for in our houses. You are aware of the critical times we live in and how easily a slight imprudence can have dire consequences.

I do want to honor your request and thus spare both you and me some serious unpleasantness or, better still, help us all to do the greatest possible good to the youngsters whom Divine Providence will entrust to our care. Hence these few directives and advice. I hope you will observe them, for they will be very helpful to you in the sacred and difficult task of religious, moral, and academic education.

In general, the educational method we must follow is the *preventive* system,[2] which aims at motivating our pupils to do what we ask of them with no external force on our part. In other words, this system means that we must never use *coercive means.* Always and only, persuasion and kindness.

Since, however, our human nature, too easily prone to evil, must at times be severely curbed, I think it best to offer you some means which I hope, with God's help, will bring us consoling results. First and foremost, if we wish to be known as true friends of our pupils when we demand they carry out their duties, you must never forget that you represent the parents of those dear young people who have always been the tender object of my concern, study, and priestly ministry, as well as of our Salesian Congregation. And so, if you are to be true fathers to your pupils, you too must have a father's heart and never resort to *repression* or to *punishments* which are unreasonable and unjust. You must also show that you are being forced to punish and cannot shirk your responsibility.

I now intend to point out the true reasons which must induce you to *repression* and which punishments may be used and who should use them.

I. Punish Only as a Last Resort

How often in my long career, my dear sons, have I had to convince myself of this important truth! It is certainly much easier to lose one's temper than to be patient, to threaten a child rather than to persuade him. Let me say also that it better suits our impatience and our pride to punish those who resist us than to correct them and bear with them firmly and kindly. The charity I am suggesting is that shown by St. Paul to his new Christian converts to our Lord's religion; he was often driven to tears, but he would pray for them whenever he felt they were less docile and less responsive to his anxious care.

And so I ask all directors to be the first to correct our dear children with fatherliness, and let it be done in private, or as we say, *in camera caritatis*. They are never to reprimand anyone in public unless it be a case of forestalling or repairing scandal.

If the first admonition brings on no improvement, let the director consult with another superior who may have some influence over the culprit. Finally let him discuss it with the Lord. I would like the Salesian to be always like Moses, who strove to placate the Lord when He became justly indignant with His people Israel. It is my experience that punishment summarily given without first trying other means rarely does any good. The heart, says St. Gregory, is an impregnable castle, and no one can force his way into it; it can be taken only by love and gentleness. Be firm in pursuing good and averting evil, but always with gentleness and prudence. Be perseverant and lovable, and you will see that God will give you mastery over even the least docile hearts. I know that this demands a perfection not commonly found in teachers and assistants, especially younger ones. They do not want to accept children as they should but prefer to use physical punishments. Thus they get nowhere. Either they let the situation get out of hand, or they deal out punishments whether they are merited or not.

That is why we often see evil spreading and breeding discontent even among the better students, while the one who should be correcting the situation has become powerless to do any good. Here again I must rely upon my own personal experience. I have often come across some youngsters so stubbornly opposed to the very notion of being good that they have made me lose any hope for their improvement, forcing me to take severe measures with them; and only kindness won them over. We sometimes think that this type of boy is not profiting from our correction, while actually his heart is strongly prompting him to follow our lead. We would let him go to the devil by an unwarranted severity on our part and by expecting the culprit to take *instant* and *decisive* steps to amend his behavior. Let me say first of all that he probably believes he does not deserve such a severe punishment for the fault he committed more through light-mindedness than malice. I have often summoned such disruptive youngsters, treated them kindly, and asked them why they were so intractable. Their defense was that they were being picked on or that they were being hounded by one superior or another. Later, I had to admit, a calm, unbiased investigation of the matter revealed that their guilt was appreciably diminished if not totally wiped away. This leads me to say with some pain that we ourselves have always had our share of responsibility for their guilt. I have also noticed that teachers who demanded of their pupils silence, punishment, exactness, prompt and unquestioning obedience were also the very ones who took no heed of the sound advice which I and other superiors were obliged to give them. I have also become convinced that those teachers who forgive nothing in their pupils usually absolve themselves of every fault. Therefore, if we wish to know how to command, let us first know how to obey, and let us endeavor to make ourselves loved more than feared.

When the time comes for us to change tactics, however, and *repression* becomes necessary, since certain traits in our pupils can be controlled only with severity, we must know how to act without showing the slightest sign of passion. Hence flows my second recommendation, which I call:

II. Choose a Favorable Time to Reprimand

Everything in its own time, says the Holy Spirit. And my advice to you is this: when, sadly, we are forced to reprimand we also need great prudence to choose the moment when the punishment will prove helpful. The soul's ailments require at least as much care as those of the body. Nothing is more dangerous than a remedy ill applied or applied at the wrong time. A skillful physician bides his time until the patient is able to handle the medication, and waits for the favorable time. We, too, will be able to know the right time only by experience permeated by goodness of heart. First and foremost, wait until you are in control of yourself. Do not let it appear that you are acting out of caprice or anger, for then you will forfeit your authority and the punishment will prove harmful.

Recall the well known dictum of Socrates to a slave who had displeased him: "If I were not angry, I would strike you." These young observers of ours, our pupils, can tell from the slightest flush of the face or our tone of voice whether it is zeal or heat of anger that gives rise to that passion within us. That is all that we need to wipe out any good which might result from punishment, for, young as they are, our pupils realize that reason alone has the right to punish them.

In the second place, never punish a boy at the moment of his fault, lest, unable then and there to admit his guilt or overcome his resentment, or even realize that he deserves punishment, he may turn bitter and behave even worse. You must give him time to reflect, to return to his senses, to become aware of his wrong and of the justice and need of punishment, and thus allow himself to benefit from it. I am always reminded of how our Lord chose to deal with St. Paul when the latter was "still breathing murderous threats" against the Christians. It seems to me that the Lord was leaving us, too, the rule to follow when we come across certain stubborn hearts rebelling against our wills. Jesus in His goodness did not strike Saul down *immediately*. He threw him to the ground only after a long journey, after he had had time to reflect upon his mission and was far from anyone who might strengthen his resolve to persecute the Christians. It was there, at the gates of Damascus, that Jesus showed Himself in all His authority and might; with gentle forcefulness He opened Saul's mind to see his error. It was precisely at that moment that his attitude changed, and from persecutor he became the Apostle of the Gentiles, a vessel of election. I would like my dear Salesians to form themselves after this divine model, so that with enlightened patience and solicitous love, they may in God's name await *the opportune moment* to correct their pupils.

III. Do Not Make It Appear That You Are Acting Out of Anger

It is difficult when punishing to maintain that necessary calm which will eliminate all doubt that one is trying to assert his authority or to give vent to his anger. The more spitefully we act, the less aware we are of it. The fatherly heart that we should have condemns such behavior. Let us look upon the pupils under our care as our own children. Shying away from anything that might smack of domineering, let us place ourselves at their service like Jesus, who came among us to obey rather than to command. Let our only authority over them be to serve them with increased dedication. Thus did Jesus act toward His apostles, tolerating their ignorance, rudeness, and shaky fidelity, reaching out to sinners with such ease and friendliness as to astonish some people, practically to scandalize others, and to kindle in many the blessed hope of receiving divine pardon. Hence he tells us to learn from Him to be "meek and humble of heart." Once these pupils have become our children, let us banish all anger when we must correct their failings, or at least so restrain it as to make it seem to disappear. Let there be no vexation in our souls, no contempt in our eyes, no cutting remarks on our lips. Rather, let us show compassion for the present and hope for the future. In this manner you will prove to be true fathers, and your correction will be genuine.

In particularly serious situations, commending oneself humbly to God will help much more than a storm of words which, on the one hand, will bring nothing but harm to the listeners and, on the other hand, will be of no advantage to those who deserve them. Let us call to mind how our divine Redeemer forgave that town which had barred His entrance, despite the charge by those two zealous apostles of His that His honor had been slighted; they would gladly have wished to see Him blast them with well-deserved punishment. This self-control the Holy Spirit commends to us in those sublime words of David: "Be angry and sin not." If we sometimes see our work as fruitless and all our efforts reaping nothing but thorns and thistles, believe me, my dear friends, the blame must fall upon a defective system of discipline. I know this is not the time to expand upon this somber, down-to-earth lesson which God once taught His prophet Elijah, who, I would say, had something in common with us in his eagerness for God's

Appendix B

cause and his rash zeal to repress the scandals that he saw multiplying in the house of Israel. Your superiors can discuss it at length with you as we read it in the book of Kings. I will just quote the closing passage, which is so relevant for us: "The Lord was not in the wind," which St. Teresa interprets as, "Let nothing upset you."

Our dear, meek St. Francis de Sales, as you know, had made a strict rule for himself that his tongue should not speak when his heart was in turmoil. "I fear," he used to say, "that I will lose in fifteen minutes the little sweetness I have striven for twenty years to accumulate, drop by drop, like dew, in the vessel of my poor heart. The bee takes several months to prepare the honey that a person can swallow in one gulp. Besides, what is the use of speaking to one who is not listening?" Reproved one day for having treated with undue kindness a boy who had had a bad run-in with his mother in a serious matter, he replied, *"This lad was in no condition to benefit by my corrections because the bad attitude of his heart had deprived him of reason and good sense. A sharp reprimand would have done him no good and would have hurt me as badly by making me act like one who drowns in an attempt to save others."* These words of our admirable patron, gentle and wise educator of the heart that he was, I have deliberately emphasized to bring them to your attention, that you may all the more readily impress them into your memory.

In certain cases it may help to remark to someone in the culprit's hearing how sad it is that sometimes people lose all sense of reason and self-respect even to the point of inviting punishment. It also helps to withhold all the usual signs of trust and friendship from one unless you realize that he needs a word of comfort. Often enough the Lord has consoled me by this simple stratagem. Public reprimand must be the last resort. Sometimes you may ask another person with influence to speak to the offender and tell him what you would like to say yourself but cannot. He may move the lad to put aside his embarrassment and be ready to talk to you. For this, choose someone to whom the boy can more freely open his aching heart than to you, either because he fears you will not believe him or because pride tells him he should not talk to you. Let these stratagems be like the disciples whom Jesus used to send before Him to prepare His way.

Make it clear to the lad that you are not suggesting anything more than what is reasonable and necessary. Try to put it in such a way that the pupil will end up blaming himself, and then all there is left for you to do is mitigate the punishment which he is ready to accept. My final recommendation to you in this serious matter is that, once you have managed to win over this stubborn soul, please do not just leave him with the hope that you have forgiven him, but reassure him that by his good conduct he can wipe out the bad name which his misbehavior has warranted.

IV. Always Leave the Culprit with the Hope of Pardon

We must always ease the anxiety and fear aroused by correction and put in a word of comfort. To forget and to make a youngster forget the dark hours of his mistakes is the supreme art of a good educator. We do not read that Jesus reminded Mary Magdalene of her past failings, and it was with the tenderest fatherly delicacy that He led St. Peter to admit his guilt and rid himself of his weakness. A child needs to know that his superior has high hopes for his betterment and thus to feel his superior's kindly hand steering him back to the path of virtue. Indeed, we obtain more with a friendly glance, with a word of encouragement, which arouse confidence in a lad's heart, than with a flood of reprimands which only upset him and crush his spirit. I have seen this method achieve true conversions which would otherwise have been deemed utterly impossible. I know that some of

Appendix B

my own dearest sons are not ashamed to admit that they were won over to the Congregation, and so to God, by this means. All youngsters have their crises, as you too have had your own. Heaven help us if we do not make an effort to aid them over these moments swiftly and blamelessly. At times just letting them know that we do not think they acted maliciously is enough to prevent them from falling into the same fault. They may be guilty, but they do not want to be seen that way. How blessed we are if we can learn to apply also these means to educate these poor hearts! Be assured, my dear sons, that this art, which appears so easy and not conducive to good results, will make your ministry useful and win over to you certain hearts which were and would long continue to be incapable not only of happy achievement but also of any hope of improvement.

V. Which Punishments May Be Used, and by Whom

Are punishments never allowed? My dear sons, I realize that the Lord chose to compare Himself to a "vigilant rod," *virga vigilans,* so as to deter us from sin also by fear of punishment. We too, therefore, can and must sparingly and wisely follow the pattern which He traces out for us in this effective metaphor. Yes, let us use this *rod,* but let us know how to use it reasonably and lovingly, so that our correction be such as may bring improvement.

We must bear in mind that, while force punishes crime, it does not cure the criminal. Just as a plant does not thrive on harsh or violent treatment, neither is the will trained by being subjected to excessive strain. Here are some punishments which are the *only* ones I wish us to use. One of the most effective kinds of moral force is the superior's unhappy, stern, and grieved look, which tells the culprit—little heart as he may have—that he has shamed himself and may move him to feel sorry and do better. Correction is to be private and fatherly, with no excessive reproaching, but rather impressing the culprit with his family's disappointment and the hope of reward. In the long run he will feel compelled to show himself thankful and even generous. Should he slip again, let us not run short on kindness, but move on to more serious and decisive admonishment which will enable him to recognize the vast difference between the way he is acting and the way he is being treated. Let us show him how he is repaying all the gracious efforts being made to save him from disgrace and punishment. No humiliating words, however. Let him know that we have not lost hope for him but are ready at any time to let bygones be bygones the moment he gives signs of improving his behavior.

More serious infractions may be punished in some of these ways: eating supper standing in one's place or at a separate table or in the middle of the dining room or, last of all, by the door. But in all these cases see to it that the culprit gets the same food as his companions. A grave punishment is to deprive him of recreation, but he is not to be exposed to the sun or inclement weather so that he would be harmed by it.

To ignore him in the classroom for *one day,* and no more than that, can also be a serious punishment. In the meantime he should be encouraged to mend his ways. Now, what do I think of *punishment work?* Unfortunately it is all too commonly used. I have consulted some of the most renowned educators to learn what they have to say about it. Some, I found, approve, while others discount it as worthless and hazardous to both pupil and teacher. I leave it up to your own discretion, but I cite the risk you run. A teacher can easily go to extremes to no purpose at all, while the pupil is free to complain that he is being picked on and thus gain the sympathy of others. *Punishment work* remedies nothing; it is always a penalty and humiliation. I know of one confrere who used to assign as *punishment* memorizing some lines of sacred and secular poetry; by such a useful means he obtained greater attention and some intellectual advantage. But

Appendix B

this only confirms that "all things work for good" in those who seek only God, His glory, and the salvation of souls. This confrere of yours achieved conversions with *punishment work,* but I recognize it as a special divine blessing not only rare but unique. He succeeded only because he made his kindness evident.

Never are you to use the so-called *reflection closet.*[3] [A poor translation of Italian *camerino* meaning *little room.* A better expression would be *reflection room.* Au.] The anger and dejection caused by this sort of treatment can thrust a child into all sorts of problems. The devil uses this punishment to exercise a most violent power over the child, driving him into doing grave offenses, as though in revenge on the one who has punished him in that manner.[4]

Our consideration of punishments has so far concentrated on violations of school rules. In the sad event, however, that a pupil gives grave scandal or offends the Lord, he is to be referred immediately to the director, who will prudently take the measures which he judges will be effective and opportune. Should this pupil be deaf to these thoughtful measures for his improvement and continue to give bad example and scandal to others, he should be summarily dismissed, his good name being protected as much as possible. This can be done by suggesting that the lad ask his family to withdraw him from the school or by directly advising the family to change schools in the hope that their son will do better elsewhere. This kind of thoughtfulness is always effective, and even in certain very painful situations it leaves both pupils and families with grateful memories.

Finally, let me tell you again who is to prescribe punishments and when and how he is to do so.

It must always be the director, though he is not to appear to do so. His role is to give private corrections, since he can more easily penetrate less docile hearts. He is also to administer general and public corrections. It is also his role to apply the punishment, though ordinarily he is not the one to threaten or carry it out. Therefore I wish that no one should take it on himself to punish without the previous counsel or approval of the director, who alone will determine the time, extent, and manner of punishment. No one is to evade this loving dependence, nor to seek excuses for avoiding the surveillance of the director. There are to be no excuses to depart from this most important rule. Obey my recommendation, and God will bless and console you for your virtue.

Remember that education is a matter of the heart, of which God alone is the master, and that we can achieve nothing unless God teaches us the art and hands us the key. Hence let us use all means, including our entire and humble dependence upon Him, to become masters of that fortress which locks itself off from all severity and harshness. Let us strive to make ourselves loved, to instill a sense of duty and of holy fear of God, and we shall see hearts open to us with surprising ease; they will join us in singing the praises and blessing of Him who chose to make Himself our model, our way, our example in all things, especially in the education of the young.

Pray for me, and believe me always in the Most Sacred Heart of Jesus

Your most loving father and friend,

Father JOHN BOSCO

APPENDIX B

1. We have based our translation on the critical edition by José Manuel Prellezo, published in *Ricerche storiche salesiane,* V (1986), 263–308, rather than on the version offered as document 1 in the appendix of the Italian edition of this volume, pp. 439–447. Included in Father Prellezo's treatment is a discussion of the manuscripts (pp. 274–284) and possible authorship (pp. 266–268). [Editor]

Appendix B

2. See *Regulations of the Houses of the Society of St. Francis de Sales.* [Footnote in the original]
3. Should it happen by rare exception and extreme necessity that one of our schools should feel that it must use the closet, let me state some precautions I would like used.

   The catechist, or another superior, must often look in on the poor culprit and, with kind and compassionate words, seek to pour a little oil upon that irritated heart. He should sympathize with the lad's sorry situation and strive to let him understand that all his superiors are sorry that they had to use such an extreme measure. Let him try to lead the boy to ask for pardon, to indicate his readiness to obey, to ask for a chance to show his improvement. The moment this punishment seems to be effective, let it even be cut short. Then you can be assured you have won the lad's heart.

   Punishment is meant to be a remedy, and we must be ready to stop it as soon as we have achieved our twofold end: to eliminate evil and to prevent its return. By pardoning we also bring precious healing to the lad's distressed heart; he sees that he has not lost his superior's good will, and he will all the more readily do what he ought. [Footnote in the original]

   The expression *reflection closet* is a poor translation of the Italian word *camerino*, which means "small room." The better expression would be *reflection room.* [Writer's observation]
4. Neither teachers nor assistants are ever to put a culprit out of the classroom. In breaches of discipline let them send him with another pupil to the director. [Footnote in the original]

C Letter from Rome*

Rome, 10 May 1884

My dear sons in Jesus Christ,

    Whether I am at home or away I am always thinking of you. I have only one wish, to see you happy both in this world and in the next. It was this idea, this wish of mine, that made me write this letter. Being away from you, and not being able to see or hear you, upsets me more than you can imagine. For that reason I would have liked to write these few lines to you a week ago, but constant work prevented me. And so, although I shall be back very soon, I want to send you this letter in advance, since I cannot yet be with you in person. These words come from someone who loves you very dearly in Christ Jesus, someone who has the duty of speaking to you with the freedom of a father. You'll let me do that, won't you? And you will pay attention to what I am going to say to you, and put it into practice.

    I have said that you are always and exclusively in my thoughts. Well, a couple of evenings ago I had gone to my room, and while

    I was preparing for bed I began to say the prayers my good mother taught me, and whether I simply fell asleep or became distracted

    I don't know, but it seemed that two of the former pupils of the Oratory in its early days were standing there before me. One of them came up to me, greeted me warmly, and said: "Do you recognize me, Don Bosco?"

    "Of course, I do", I answered.

    "And do you still remember me?", the man went on.

    "I remember you and all the others. You're Valfré, and you were at the Oratory before 1870."

APPENDIX C 131

"Tell me", went on Valfré, "would you like to see the youngsters who were at the Oratory in my time?"

"Yes, let me see them", I answered, "I would like that very much."

Valfré then showed me the boys just as they had been at that time, with the same age, build and looks. I seemed to be in the old Oratory at recreation time. It was a scene full of life, full of movement, full of fun. Some were running, some were jumping, some were skipping. In one place they were playing leap-frog, in another tig, and in another a ball-game was in progress. In one corner a group of youngsters were gathered round a priest, hanging on his every word as he told them a story. In another a cleric was playing with a number of lads at "chase the donkey" and "trades". There was singing and laughing on all sides, there were priests and clerics everywhere and the boys were yelling and shouting all round them. You could see that the greatest cordiality and confidence reigned between youngsters and superiors. I was overjoyed at the sight, and Valfré said to me: "You see, closeness leads to affection, and affection brings confidence. It is this that opens hearts and the young people express everything without fear to the teachers, to the assistants and to the superiors. They become frank both in the confessional and out of it, and they will do everything they are asked by one who they know loves them."

At that moment the other past pupil, who had a white beard, came up to me and said: "Don Bosco, would you like to see and know the boys who are at the Oratory at the present time?" This man was Joseph Buzzetti.

"Yes", I replied, "it is a month since I last saw them." And he showed them to me.

I saw the Oratory and all of you in recreation. But no more could I hear the joyful shouts and singing, no longer was there the lively activity of the previous scene. In the faces and actions of many boys there was evident a weary boredom, a surliness, a suspicion, that pained me. I saw many, it is true, who ran about and played in light-hearted joy. But I saw quite a number of others on their own, leaning against the pillars, a prey to depressing thoughts. Others were on the steps or in the corridors, or up on the terraces near the garden so as to be away from the common recreation. Others were strolling about in groups, talking to each other in low tones and casting furtive and suspicious glances in every direction. Sometimes they would laugh, but with looks and smirks that would make you not only suspect but feel quite certain that St. Aloysius would have blushed to find himself in their company. Even among those who were playing, there were some so listless that it was clear they were not enjoying their games.

"Do you see your boys?", asked my former pupil.

"I can see them", I replied with a sigh.

"How different they are from what we used to be", went on the past pupil.

"Too true! What an apathetic recreation!"

"This is what gives rise to the coldness of so many in approaching the sacraments, to neglect of the prayers in church and elsewhere; to their reluctance to be in a place where Divine Providence heaps every possible blessing on their bodies, their souls and their minds. This is why so many do not follow their vocation, why they are ungrateful to their superiors, why they are secretive and grumble, with all the other regrettable consequences."

"I see, I understand," I said. "But how can we bring these youngsters to life again, so that we can get back to the liveliness, the happiness, the warmth of the old days?"

"With charity!"

"With charity? But don't my boys get enough love? You know how I love them. You know how much I have suffered and put up with for them these forty years, and how much I endure and suffer even now. How many hardships, how many

Appendix C

humiliations, how much opposition, how many persecutions to give them bread, a home, teachers, and especially to provide for the salvation of their souls. I have done everything I possibly could for them; they are the object of all my affections."

"I am not referring to you."

"Then to whom are you referring? To those who take my place? To the rectors, the prefects, the teachers, the assistants? Don't you see that they are martyrs to study and work, and how they burn out their young lives for those Divine Providence has entrusted to them?"

"I can see all that and I am well aware of it, but it is not enough; the best thing is missing."

"All right then. What is it that is missing?"

"That the youngsters should not only be loved, but that they themselves should know that they are loved."

"But have they not got eyes in their heads? Have they no intelligence? Don't they see how much is done for them, and all of it out of love?"

"No, I repeat: it is not enough."

"Well, what else is needed?"

"By being loved in the things they like, through taking part in their youthful interests, they are led to see love in those things too which they find less attractive, such as discipline, study and self-denial, and so learn to do these things too with love."

"I'm afraid you'll have to explain that more clearly."

"Look at the youngsters in recreation."

I looked, and then asked: "Well what is special about it?"

"You've been educating young people for so many years and you don't understand! Look harder! Where are our Salesians?"

I looked, and I saw that very few priests and clerics mixed with the boys, and fewer still were joining in their games. The superiors were no longer the heart and soul of the recreation. Most of them were walking up and down, chatting among themselves without taking any notice of what the pupils were doing. Others looked on at the recreation but paid little heed to the boys. Others supervised from afar, not noticing whether anyone was doing something wrong. Some did take notice but only rarely, and then in a threatening manner. Here and there a Salesian did try to mix with a group of boys, but I saw that the latter were bent on keeping their distance from teachers and superiors.

Then my friend continued: "In the old days at the Oratory, were you not always among the boys, especially during recreation? Do you remember those wonderful years? They were a foretaste of heaven, a period of which we have fond memories, because then love was the rule and we had no secrets from you."

"Yes, indeed! Everything was a joy for me then, and the boys used to rush to get near me and talk to me; they were anxious to hear my advice and put it into practice. But don't you see that now with these never-ending interviews, business matters, and my poor health I cannot do it any more."

"Well and good; but if you cannot do it, why don't your Salesians follow the example you gave? Why don't you insist, why don't you demand, that they treat the boys as you used to do?"

"I do. I talk till I'm blue in the face, but unfortunately not everyone nowadays feels like working as hard as we used to."

"And so by neglecting the lesser part they waste the greater, meaning all the work they put in. Let them like what pleases the youngsters and the youngsters will come to like what pleases the superiors. In this way their work will be made easy. The reason for the present change in the Oratory is that many of the boys no longer have confidence in their superiors. There was a time when all hearts were wide open to their superiors, when the boys loved them and gave them prompt obedience. But now the superiors are thought of precisely as superiors and no longer as fathers, brothers and friends; they are

Appendix C

feared and little loved. And so if you want everyone to be of one heart and soul again for the love of Jesus you must break down this fatal barrier of mistrust, and replace it with a happy spirit of confidence. Then obedience will guide the pupil as a mother guides her baby; and the old peace and happiness will reign once again in the Oratory."

"How then are we to set about breaking down this barrier?"

"By a friendly informal relationship with the boys, especially in recreation. You cannot have affection without this familiarity, and where affection is not evident there can be no confidence. If you want to be loved, you must make it clear that you love. Jesus Christ made himself little with the little ones and bore our weaknesses. He is our master in the matter of the friendly approach. The teacher who is seen only in the classroom is a teacher and nothing more; but if he joins in the pupils' recreation he becomes their brother. If someone is only seen preaching from the pulpit it will be said that he is doing no more and no less than his duty, whereas if he says a good word in recreation it is heard as the word of one who loves. How many conversions have been brought about by a few words whispered in the ear of a youngster while he is playing. One who knows he is loved loves in return, and one who loves can obtain anything, especially from the young. This confidence creates an electric current between youngsters and their superiors. Hearts are opened, needs and weaknesses made known. This love enables superiors to put up with the weariness, the annoyance, the ingratitude, the troubles that youngsters cause. Jesus Christ did not crush the bruised reed nor quench the smouldering flax. He is your model. Then you will no longer see anyone working for his own glory; you will no longer see anyone punishing out of wounded self-love; you will not see anyone neglecting the work of supervision through jealousy of another's popularity; you won't hear people running others down so as to be looked up to by the boys: those who exclude all other superiors and earn for themselves nothing but contempt and hypocritical flattery; people who let their hearts be stolen by one individual and neglect all the other boys to cultivate that particular one. No one will neglect his strict duty of supervision for the sake of his own ease and comfort; no one will fail through human respect to reprimand those who need reprimanding. If we have this true love, we shall not seek anything other than the glory of God and the good of souls. When this love languishes, things no longer go well. Why do people want to replace love with cold rules? Why do the superiors move away from the observance of the rules Don Bosco has given them? Why the replacement little by little of loving and watchful prevention by a system which consists in framing laws? Such laws either have to be sustained through punishment and so create hatred and cause unhappiness or, if they are not enforced, cause the superiors to be despised and bring about serious disorders. This is sure to happen if there is no friendly relationship. So if you want the Oratory to return to the happiness of old, then bring back the old system: let the superior be all things to all, always ready to listen to any boy's complaints or doubts, always alert to keep a paternal eye on their conduct, all heart to seek the spiritual and temporal good of those Divine Providence has entrusted to him. Then hearts will no longer be closed and deadly subterfuge will no longer hold sway. The superiors should be unbending only in the case of immoral conduct. It is better to run the risk of expelling someone who is innocent than to keep someone who causes others to sin. Assistants should make it a strict duty in conscience to refer to the superiors whatever they know to be an offence against God."

Then I asked a question: "And what is the best way of achieving this friendly relationship, this kind of love and confidence?"

"The exact observance of the rules of the house."

"Nothing else?"

Appendix C

"At a dinner the best dish is a hearty welcome."

"With that my past pupil finished speaking, and I went on looking at that recreation with great displeasure. Little by little I felt oppressed by a great weariness that became worse at every moment. Eventually it got so bad that I could resist no longer, and I shook myself and woke up. I found myself standing beside my bed. My legs were so swollen and hurt so much that I could not stand up any longer. It was very late and I went to bed, resolved to write these lines to my sons."

I wish I did not have these dreams, they tire me so much. The following day I was dead tired, and I could hardly wait for the hour to come to go to bed that evening. But I was hardly in bed when the dream began again. Before me once again was the playground, with the boys at present at the Oratory and the same past pupil as before. I began to question him.

"I'll let my Salesians know what you have told me, but what should I say to the boys of the Oratory?"

"Tell them", he said, "to realize how much the superiors, the teachers, the assistants, plan and wear themselves out for love of them, since they would not sacrifice themselves so much if they didn't love them. Let them never forget that humility is the source of all peace of mind; let them be able to put up with each other's shortcomings, because there is no perfection in this world, only in heaven. Tell them not to grumble because it freezes the heart. But especially, tell them to live in the holy grace of God. If you are not at peace with God, you cannot be at peace with yourself, nor with others."

"Are you telling me then that among my boys there are some who are not at peace with God?"

"Among other reasons you already know, this is the principal cause of bad spirit. There is no need for me to tell you that you must do something about it. The one without trust is the one with secrets to guard, the one who is afraid the secrets will become known and bring him shame and trouble. At the same time, if his heart is not at peace with God he will be a prey to restless anxiety, intolerant of obedience, and get upset over nothing. Everything seems to go wrong for him, and because he has no love himself he thinks the superiors do not love him."

"But see here, my friend; look how many go to confession and communion here at the Oratory."

"It is true that many go to confession, but what is *radically* lacking in the confessions of so many youngsters is a firm resolution. They tell their sins but they are always the same, always the same occasions, the same bad habits, the same acts of disobedience, the same neglect of duty. This goes on, month in, month out, even for years and some even continue in this way till they leave school. These confessions are worth little or nothing, and so they do not restore peace, and if a youngster in that state were to be called before God's judgement seat, it would be a serious matter indeed. But in comparison with the whole group in the house they are only a few. Look." And he pointed them out to me.

I looked, and I saw those boys one by one. There were not many, but in them I saw things that brought profound bitterness to my soul. I do not want to put such things in writing, but when I come back I want to have a word with each one about what I saw. For the moment I limit myself to saying that it is time to pray and make firm resolutions, with facts and not just words, so as to show that the Comollos, the Dominic Savios, the Besuccos and the Saccardis are still among us.

I put a final question to my friend: "Have you anything else to tell me?"

"Preach to all, young and old alike, that they must remember they are children of Mary Help of Christians. Tell them she has gathered them here to take them away from the dangers of the world, so that they may love one another as brothers and give glory to God and to her by their good behaviour. Tell them that it is Our Lady who provides them with bread and the means to study, by endless graces and wonders. Remind them that they are at the vigil of the feast of their holy Mother, so that with her help that barrier of mistrust will fall which has been raised between boys and superiors by the devil, who knows how to use it to ruin certain souls."

"And will we be successful in breaking down this barrier?"

"Certainly you will, as long as young and old are ready to put up with some small mortifications for love of Mary and do what I have told you."

Meanwhile I continued to watch my youngsters, but at the sight of those I had seen heading for eternal damnation I experienced such heartache that I awoke. I still have to tell you many important things that I saw, but I have neither time nor opportunity at present.

And now I must finish. Do you know what this poor old man who has spent his whole life for his dear boys wants from you? Nothing else than, due allowances being made, we should go back to the happy days of the Oratory of old: the days of affection and Christian confidence between boys and superiors; the days when we accepted and put up with difficulties for the love of Jesus Christ; the days when hearts were open with a simple candour; days of love and real joy for everyone. I want the consolation and hope that you will promise to do everything I desire for the good of your souls.

You do not realize how lucky you are in having come to the Oratory. I declare before God: it is enough for a young person to enter a Salesian house for Our Lady to take him under her special care. Let us all agree on this then: may the charity of those who command and the charity of those who must obey cause the spirit of St. Francis de Sales to reign among us. My dear children, the time is coming when I will have to tear myself away from you and leave for eternity. (*Secretary's note:* at this point Don Bosco broke off the dictation; his eyes filled with tears, not of sorrow but because of the inexpressible affection that was evident from his face and voice; after a few moments he went on.) "And so I want to leave you, my dear priests and brothers and my dearest boys, on the road the Lord himself wants you to follow. For this purpose the Holy Father, whom I saw on Friday 9 May, sends you his blessing from the bottom of his heart."

I will be with you on the feast of Mary Help of Christians, before the statue of our loving Mother. I want this feast to be celebrated with full solemnity, and that Fr. Lazzero and Fr. Marchisio see to it that you have a good time in the dining-room as well. The feast of Mary Help of Christians should be a prelude to the eternal feast that we will all celebrate one day together in heaven.

With much love, your friend in Christ Jesus.

Father JOHN BOSCO

APPENDIX C

* *Constitutions of the Society of St. Francis de Sales,* 1985, 254. *Atti del Capitolo della Pia Società Salesiana,* 1920 no. 1, (24 June), 40–48.